Television is good for your kids

Máire Messenger Davies

First published 1989 by
Hilary Shipman Limited
19 Framfield Road
Highbury
London N5 1UU

British Library Cataloguing in Publication Data
Messenger Davies, Máire
    Television is good for your kids.
    1. Children's television programmes
    I. Title
    791.45'5

ISBN 0-948096-14-4
         0-948096-15-2 pbk

Cover design by David Bennett

Typeset by Florencetype Ltd, Kewstoke, Avon
Printed and bound by Biddles Limited
Guildford & King's Lynn

Contents

The author

Máire Messenger Davies is a psychologist
and a journalist. Her first degree was in
English, and in 1988 she was awarded a
doctorate for her research into the effects of
television camera techniques on attention
and memory. Author of *The Breastfeeding
Book* (Century) and, with two co-authors,
Baby Language (Unwin Hyman), she is an
adviser and regular contributor to *Parents*
magazine. She has written extensively on
children and television for national newspapers and the *Times Educational Supplement*, and has regularly reviewed children's
television for *The Listener*. She has acted
as research consultant to the British Film
Institute and is a member of the steering
group of British Action for Children's Television. She is married to a journalist. In the
company of their four children, aged nine to
eighteen, they have watched and enjoyed a
great deal of television.

Acknowledgements

Many people have helped in gathering information for this book. Some of them have written books and articles themselves – and credit is given to them in the references and bibliography. But a number have been particularly helpful in allowing me access to material or putting me in touch with other sources. I would particularly like to thank: Dr Mallory Wober of the Independent Broadcasting Authority Research Department; Andrew Hemming and his colleagues in the BBC's Broadcasting Research Department; Roy Thompson, Deputy Head of the BBC Children's Department; and the staff of the Children's Department, especially the two producers who allowed me access to their programme material, Chris Tandy and Anne Gobey. I should also like to thank Tony Hart for telling me about his work with *Hartbeat*. Frank Flynn, Education Officer for BBC Schools Television and Wendy Tobitt, BBC Schools Press Officer, contributed valuable information for the chapter on television in the classroom, as did Diane Lewis, Deputy Head of Brooklands Infant School in London and her class of top infants. Lewis Rudd of Central Television and Clare Mulholland and Sue Elliott of the IBA have been extremely helpful in giving me information about ITV children's programmes.

Thanks are also due to Philip Simpson, Cary Bazalgette and colleagues in the Education Department of the British Film Institute, and David Buckingham, of the Institute of Education, University of London, who directed me to many sources of relevant information, particularly about the value of media education in school and at home. Carrick James, of Carrick James Market Research, Elisabeth Sweeney of the Children's Research Unit and Jane Browning and the staff of The Research Business, were all extremely generous in allowing me access to their market research on children's tastes and viewing habits. Special thanks are due to Peter and Dympna LeRasle for help with word-processing.

I would like to thank all the children who contributed material for this book, including my own. I particularly want to pay tribute to all the many people – producers, performers, writers, technicians – who have helped to fill my children's childhood with interest, amusement and occasionally enchantment, through the children's television programmes that we have enjoyed over the last 18 years. Television is a lucrative and competitive business and it can be difficult to make your name and your fortune if you stick to making simple series designed to extend the horizons and imaginations of very small people, living in cramped urban conditions, who can't safely play on the streets any more. It can be hard to survive in a competitive broadcasting system if you passionately believe in spending as much money on good drama for children as on drama for adults – even though you may 'only' get an audience of two or three million for it.

Nevertheless, there are many parents, teachers and others who care about the needs of children, who want talented broadcasters to go on valuing children as a worthwhile audience for their programmes. There are still a great number of such talented people working in British television, and, I hope, there are more to come. This book is dedicated to them.

Máire Messenger Davies

1 | Television is good for your kids

There are many people who will think that the title of this book is a heresy. We have all heard, perhaps from newspapers, perhaps from teachers, perhaps from television itself, that television is bad for children. We may be unhappy about how our own children use TV, we may feel guilty because we think they should be doing something more 'improving'. Whenever the topic of television and children becomes the subject of popular debate, it is the bad that we hear about. Even the Prince of Wales, whose own children, we have read, enjoy watching television, chose to focus on the unpleasantness of violent videos when he opened London's new Museum of the Moving Image in the autumn of 1988. But there is another, good, side to children's relationship with television and that – unfashionably – is what this book aims to show.

Children's rights

Like most of their contemporaries, the Prince and Princess of Wales seem to be conscientious and caring parents. Something else that conscientious and caring parents could be concerned about is the right of children to good television programmes of their own. The year 1988 saw the summary removal of regular young children's programmes from Channel 4 when its new Chief Executive, Michael Grade, took over. It saw the end of the 25-year run of *Play School* on BBC1 – replaced, admittedly, by another well-made pre-

1

school series, *Playbus*, but still one made outside the BBC and on a limited-term contract. At the Edinburgh Television Festival, a senior executive in London Weekend Television complained about the amount of money spent by ITV on children's programmes; proposed Government legislation on broadcasting indicates that commercial television, until now carrying as high a reputation as the BBC for quality programmes, will no longer have a public service duty to 'educate and inform'. The legislation includes no recommendations about children's programmes.

Children's programmes and children's needs have been in the front line of the attack on public service broadcasting values during the year in which this book was being written, and many worries have been expressed about children's programmes disappearing, or going 'downmarket'. It's thought that we may be inundated with 'a flood of cheap, American cartoons', as one letter-writer to *Radio Times* put it, when the ending of *Play School* was announced. British broadcasting is in the process of becoming 'deregulated' – that is, no longer primarily under the control of publicly appointed bodies, such as the Independent Broadcasting Authority (IBA), with a responsibility to see that TV 'informs and educates' as well as 'entertains'; commercial television in future will be 'lightly' controlled by the more commercially oriented Independent Television Commission. Access to the airwaves is becoming an increasingly commercial commodity, to be sold to anyone who can afford the enormous financial outlay required to set up new cable and satellite TV services; an outlay that can only be recouped by advertising, which in turn is attracted by big audiences.

Many people fear that broadcasting could cease to be seen as a public service, aiming to meet the needs of everyone, including minorities and people without spending power, like children. Clare Mulholland, Deputy Director of Television at the IBA, pointed out, in an interview in *Broadcast* magazine (30 September 1988):

Children's programming is largely subsidised by other income-earning programming and, apart from internationally appealing animation series, it is not much of a moneymaker.

Another possible problem of this deregulated system is that once programmes can be beamed into this country from abroad, by satellite, we may receive shows from countries with much laxer standards about violence and pornography than our own. How can children be protected from this?

Emphasising the positive

These are some of the worries about children and television currently being expressed. But it is important in this debate not to lose sight of the positive – and, above all, not to forget the children themselves, whose voices are seldom heard. If children's needs are to be considered in the new deregulated system of broadcasting, it's important to demonstrate that television provides experiences for children that are valuable and should be preserved and extended. People who are concerned about children but who dwell only on the negative side of the relationship between television and the young, are actually playing into the hands of those who want to dismiss children's broadcasting needs. After all, if television is always, and in every way, bad for children, the less the television service does to attract them, the better. What does it matter if we have cheap, violent cartoons for children, instead of literate (and expensive) drama? It's all television, and it's all bad, isn't it?

But television is not always and in every way bad for children – and this book is about some of the good things that have happened, and can happen, to children which seem to be associated with viewing. This is a more cautious way of putting it than the words often chosen by adverse critics of television's effects on children. It would be tempting to say that good things happen to children *as a result* of watching television. However, nearly everyone who, like me, has done research into the subject, as distinct from speaking only from their own personal experience, learns that television doesn't have a simple effect on children. It isn't spooned into them like vitamin supplements ('good' effects) or sugar ('bad' effects).

The role of the child

What children get from television depends on what children bring to it. Depending on how old they are, how bright they are, how tired they are, what sort of family they belong to, what sort of skills they already have, television will affect them differently. And the same child will react differently to television programmes at different stages in his or her life. Indeed, the same is true of vitamin supplements and sugar, which are not, in every circumstance, respectively 'good' and 'bad'. It is possible to overdose on vitamins; it is possible to suffer from a lack of the right kinds of sugar. Furthermore, anything at all that is 'put in' to human beings will be modified and changed as a result of being processed by those human beings – and the ways in which it is modified can vary, just as human beings vary.

The effects of television on children can also depend on what sort of programmes they are watching and how the programmes are made. This book looks at some of the programmes which are made for, and enjoyed by, children and discusses some of the assumptions about children which guide the producers of programmes in making their decisions. It also asks: What exactly do children watch and what do they think of it? What do they make of advertising, soap opera, cartoons, violent drama? What moves them, bores them, makes them angry, makes them think? How does television fit in with other activities in their lives? Where do they find the time for it? How aware are we of the different needs and different responses of different age groups? And within age groups, what about boys and girls?

Black children and white children? How well do the programme makers and the audience know each other? Children watch a lot of television intended for adults. What do they make of it?

Many people would answer these questions in a negative way – some of these negative arguments are looked at more closely in Chapter 4. It has been argued that television teaches children to be violent, that it makes them passive, that it takes up too much of their time, that it promotes racism or sexism or commercialism or even imperialism. In fact, we don't *know* all the effects television has. Many of these questions have simply not been put to children in any systematic way. Fears about the effects of violence or stereotyping often reflect adults' anxieties about what they think might be happening rather than anything that really is happening. Where answers have been sought, the picture often looks more reassuring.

This book aims to show this more reassuring aspect. I am aware that there is another, more negative, side, just as there is to every argument. However, we have all heard the case for the prosecution; this is the much less frequently heard case for the defence. It is only a partial defence: there is so much positive research; so much rich and creative classroom work with children studying the media; so many individual observations about television and its relationship with children's lives, that only a small proportion of it can be mentioned. Inevitably, therefore, the information in this book is selective because of the need to choose from this plethora of material.

Taking television seriously

The creative processes involved in making television for children and the moral, educational, practical and commercial decisions that have to be made in getting such programmes onto the air, are a book in themselves. This book is not an account of how children's programmes are made, nor a work of criticism about children's television. Nevertheless, one of the feelings that inform the book is the belief that children will never get, and keep, the good television that they deserve, so long as the critical attention that is lavishly afforded to books, is denied to television. An important source of cultural and social information for children will continue to be underestimated so long as television is seen by intelligent people as, at most, a necessary evil – a 'plug-in drug' to keep the kids quiet when they're not doing more 'worthy' things like playing the piano or homework.

Apart from the occasional rare critic, such as Christopher Dunkley of the *Financial Times*, television still awaits intelligent popular analysts, with an enthusiasm for the medium, who can evaluate it on its own terms and not in comparison with books or other media. Apart from rare researchers like Bob Hodge and David Tripp (whose work is described in Chapter 5), few educational thinkers attempt to test children's critical and imaginative faculties via television, rather than via exclusively literary models, and very little research of any kind has been done in Britain. Cognitive psychology, the field in which I did my own doctoral research on the effects of camera technique on learning from television, has a wealth of literature about how people understand and remember spoken and written information. There is still very little about how people deal with structured visual information, often of great narrative, technical and artistic complexity, and the effects of such structures on growing minds.

My own research explored the relationship between the long-standing grammatical rules people use for understanding and remembering verbal language, and the new 20th century 'rules' that viewers have had to learn to understand the visual techniques of television. The research found similarities between these two sets of rules; it found, for instance, that people seem to expect the structure of spoken

sentences in a TV soundtrack to map onto the structure of
the way shots are put together. If these structures did not
map onto each other – for example, where shots changed
for no reason in the middle of spoken sentences – people's
memory for what they had heard was disrupted.

Children have to learn about television rules, such as
cutting from one scene to another, or emphasising important
details by the use of close-up, as they watch, and as they
grow up. How soon do they begin to learn these rules? Do
such rules in fact exist in people's minds? The findings that I
came up with suggest that TV rules do exist – even though
people are not consciously aware of them: if you ask
viewers, for instance,to notice cuts, they can find it difficult
to do so. Nevertheless, viewers' understanding of television,
and the way what they see and hear is organised in memory,
can be consistently affected by techniques like cuts and
close-ups. My research suggested that children's reactions
are different from adults. Adolescents' memory for TV
news, for instance, was not disrupted by arbitrary cutting, as
adults' memories were. Young children's perceptions were
not affected by close-ups in the way that adults' were.
Television's way of representing the world can affect the way
growing children see the world generally. Some teachers and
other adults may be too busy complaining about violence or
late nights to stop and think about the contribution television might be making to language learning, or to perception. Television, despite being the most pervasive medium
ever known, and despite employing thousands of the most
creative and gifted people in the societies in which it
operates, is not always taken seriously as a medium worthy
of critical attention. This cannot be good for some of its
biggest fans – children.

Giving children credit

The studies and examples cited in this book have been
selected from a much greater number to be representative of

the book's main argument. Readers who want to know more
will find many invaluable sources in the bibliography, where
research referred to in the text is identified as it occurs in the
chapters. These studies unashamedly represent the good
news about television. The bad news about television has
had a fair crack of the whip. Research which shows how
children's imaginative work is enhanced by watching television, or how they can critically assess the difference
between real and fantasy violence, very rarely hits the
headlines. The creative work stimulated by television in the
classroom is rarely mentioned in the current debates about
'standards' in education. Children's own responses to TV
programmes – their generosity, their common sense, their
creativity, their scepticism – are hardly ever acknowledged.
Obviously, we shouldn't be sentimental or complacent about
the role of such a powerful medium in children's lives. But
we do need to be aware of its capacity for good, and we do
need to give children much more credit for being discriminating and creative in their reactions than has sometimes been
given in the past. For all these reasons, this book is going to
stick its neck out and say: 'Television is good for your kids'.

2 | The first side of the partnership: children

People often talk about 'children and television' without any clear definition of what they mean by either children or television. A child could be a baby who can't speak yet. It could be a toddler, still learning the rules of behaviour. It could be a primary school pupil – or even a secondary school pupil – puzzling over the skills of reading. Are we talking about boys or girls? Only children or members of a large family? Tower block dwellers or farmers' children living in remote parts of Scotland? Children with two parents, or four parents or one parent or no parents? Television, as will be discussed in more detail later, is not a simple medium. In this country, it has four main channels, with many regional variations, and an increasing number of satellite and cable channels, all with an enormous variety of output, from *Playbus*, the descendant of *Play School*, to *Panorama* via *Blind Date* and Crown Green Bowling. The position and number of television sets in different households, and the use of the video (now installed in nearly 50 per cent of British homes, and 61 per cent of households with children); the use of the remote control; the different needs and requirements of different family groups; all these and many more factors affect the relationship between 'children and television'. The relationship is thus anything but simple.

Given that about 98 per cent of all households possess at least one television set, about 43 per cent of households own more than one, with half of British households owning a video, the definition of 'children and television' clearly

embraces an enormous variety of individuals and programmes. Children vary according to social class, family
position, natural ability and degrees of parental encouragement, to name only a few possible sources of difference.
There are also certain broad areas in which children as a
group don't vary all that much, although there will still be
marked individual variations. All children go through similar
stages of growth and development, which help to determine
how they are affected by events in the world around them.
It is possible to find out what these are by the scientific study
of large groups of children, which many doctors and developmental psychologists have in fact done. Despite the
existence of a large body of research literature on child
development, many findings are not very widely applied in
discussions about the broadcast media. In deciding what is
or is not appropriate material for television viewing by
children, some knowledge of how children normally grow
and develop, and how these processes can, or cannot, be
modified by other people, is helpful.

To take a very obvious example, we could consider the
possible corrupting effects of certain sorts of obscene
language on children. (Bad language is by far the greatest
source of complaints by viewers, both to the BBC and the
IBA.) We need not worry too much if a two-month-old baby
is in the room when these words are being uttered, since
babies do not understand meanings of words, although they
can be upset by the angry feelings behind them. An 18-
month-old may happily imitate four-letter words, which is
embarrassing for you in company, but is unlikely to corrupt
him or her. The more socially confident four-year-old, by
now used to mixing with other children and aware of social
rules, may use the words more appropriately, either to fit in
with older children, or deliberately to shock. But he or she is
still unlikely to understand why the words are shocking.
Indeed, many older children may use obscene words like
'bugger' without having any idea of their true meaning.
An adolescent, who is aware of contextual importance in

defining the meanings of words, will be able to appreciate the difference between the use of bad language in a play about conditions in the Army during the First World War, and its gratuitous and inappropriate use in a chat show. In one case, it can be justified on the grounds of dramatic realism; in the other case it can be criticised as bad manners.

Thus, in any debate about bad language and children, at least two categories of children (the baby and the reasonably intelligent adolescent) are likely to be protected, by virtue of their developmental stage, from corruption. The problem can be narrowed down to how to protect naturally imitative four-year-olds or argumentative eight-year-olds from hearing and imitating words which are ugly on their lips and distressing to people around them.

A number of factors would need to be considered before we could say with certainty that, for example, an eight-year-old boy had been corrupted by bad language on television. In the first place, does he know what the words mean? If he does not, and if indignant adults draw his attention to the hidden meaning of the words – 'Don't use words like that, they're filthy' – who is the source of any possible 'corruption' that may take place? Other factors, such as how often the child is likely to hear bad language at home, or at school, also need to be taken into account, as do the child's own personality and his intentions. Is he always using words like this? Is he an habitually aggressive little boy? Or is he just one who likes to experiment with explosive-sounding words now and again? It also needs to be remembered that the baby, the child and the adolescent are not mutually exclusive categories; one grows into the others and behaviour that was unacceptable at eight may have mellowed by the time the child is 12, simply by virtue of the child maturing. Conversely, a pleasant and polite little boy, who never contradicts his parents, may become, under the influence of friends, a foul-mouthed lout when he is 14 and, at 18, a charming young man again, once he gets a decent job. The various factors that influence how children respond to televised 'bad examples' will be dealt with in more detail later. The point here is that there can be no blanket definition of the presumed 'corrupting effect' of bad language on 'children' without more precise definitions of what we mean by both 'effect' and 'children'.

Becoming a discriminating viewer: how children develop

During the first year, babies develop some important skills which enable them to make sense of the world. Where television is concerned, their visual sense is obviously crucial. Babies of a few weeks old will enjoy watching shapes and colours and listening to music and voices. During the first months visual preferences develop: faces are favourites, but young babies often enjoy looking at a picture as much as at a real face. The faces of their parents, brothers and sisters and other familiar people will soon become especially important to them. In the first six months babies also develop 'size constancy' – that is, they recognise an object or person is the same even when it's getting 'smaller' by moving further away or 'bigger' by coming nearer. They also begin to learn 'shape constancy' – the fact that an object stays the same, even when viewed from different angles (obviously an important skill for television watching, with its variety of camera angles). And, around six months, 'object constancy' will become apparent to parents: babies now demonstrate that they know an object is still there, even if they can't see it. If a ball rolls out of sight, they will look for it, and they enjoy games involving appearing and disappearing, like 'Peepbo'.

Understanding what is seen on television requires all these skills – and some others which babies don't yet have. For example, developing size constancy partly depends on a baby being able to use cues from the environment: the baby recognises that an object, such as a toy, is the same, although bigger when close, because he or she has been able to watch the object getting nearer. When the camera cuts from a distant shot of, say, a teddy bear to a closer shot of the same toy, the cue of movement is missing. The baby has no reliable way of knowing that it's still the same teddy bear. In close-up it looks like a different bigger one. But one thing babies do have, certainly by the time they are a year old, is the ability to recognise pictures of objects and to realise that they are pictures, not the thing itself. Babies in Western society are surrounded by pictures and it's likely that they learn to get used to different pictorial styles quite early. There are cultural differences in how people understand and produce pictures; people in some societies, with no experience of photography, for example, find three-dimensional pictures, using perspective, difficult to interpret. Young children, too, have difficulty with three-dimensional representations. Pre-school children do not scan pictures for meaning in the same systematic way that adults do, which means that they may need more time to make sense of a scene on television, particularly if the scenes are cluttered.

Studies of pre-school children have found that they could not match identical pictures – a task that many children's colouring books, comics and, indeed programmes like *Play School* and *Sesame Street* give plenty of practice in. Perhaps these children had not been watching enough pre-school television! This raises the serious point that, although studies of child development have identified particular average ages at which children develop certain skills, there is plenty of evidence that practice in these skills can improve them. If, for example, children have difficulty in spotting Humpty amid a pile of similar toys, their ability to scan a scene and find things they recognise can be improved with picture books and even just looking for objects round the room or garden. Concerned adults need to be aware of when children might need help to notice things in their environment, and, of course, to be aware of when they don't need help, and can spot Humpty perfectly well on their own. Television can be used in this way, just as other experiences can, although it has a major drawback compared to still pictures: the scene is constantly changing and moving.

Moving pictures may overload young children's perceptual abilities for two reasons: firstly, rapid editing can mean that there may not be enough time for a young child to scan the scene for meaningful elements; secondly, a great deal of information is left out on television, which uses editing to 'cut' from one scene to another, and to show different points of view. This requires feats of memory and the ability to follow a complex plot through constant scene changes, which will be beyond the intellectual abilities of pre-school children and probably quite a large proportion of infant school children.

As children grow up, go to school and become more used to the structures and conventions of stories, particularly through hearing and reading them, the demands made by television story-telling become more manageable. Most ten-year-olds can follow televised drama aimed at their age group and by early adolescence, many children will be guiding their parents around the bewildering complexities of *Hill Street Blues* with ease. Again, experience and familiarity with the medium can help to compensate for 'immature' perceptions so that even very young children can nowadays understand the conventions of 'montage'. One American study, carried out by Robin Smith in 1985, demonstrated that four-year-olds could supply the missing actions that had been left out at cuts between scenes, and seven-year-olds could do it even better. A recent Japanese study with two-year-olds, published in a NHK Broadcasting Culture Research Institute Report, found that children this young preferred to look at characters moving rather than at the camera moving. The idea exemplified by *Sesame Street* that young children just want to look at a rapid succession of pictures, rather than at real people moving about, is rather undermined by this study. Even as young as two, children expect what they are looking at to make sense in their terms.

Developing language

Apart from visual skills, the other major skill required to make sense of television is verbal ability. Television is so often described as a visual medium that there can be a danger of forgetting that it is a verbal medium too – often delivering material in highly complex sentences, with unfamiliar vocabulary and references, even in children's programmes. For instance, here is an extract from a sketch in a BBC children's series, broadcast in the early 1980s, and published in a book called *Plays for Laughs* by the series presenter Johnny Ball. (The book, intended to give children material for their own comedy shows, is a good example of the kinds of spin-offs for other activities that television can stimulate – more examples of these are given in Chapter 11.) The programme, called *Star Turn*, was a comedy show aimed at seven- to 11-year-olds, although many younger children would have seen it too.

> It's no good Deirdre. I'm batty over you. You've really hit me for six. My short square legs go all googly every time I see you. Pitch in with me, Deirdre, and our lives will know no boundaries.

It would be impossible for a child to make sense of this without some knowledge of cricketing terms – or at least the ability to understand the double meanings of 'pitch' and 'boundaries'. He or she would also need to know something about the convention of the 'madness' of love, and linguistically, to be able to follow the arguments expressed by the speaker – '(if you) pitch in with me (then) our lives will know no boundaries.' 'If . . . then' constructions can be difficult for young children to follow, because they require an understanding of logical processes, of cause and effect. Of course, children do learn to follow such constructions through practice, experience and, importantly, through feedback from the people around them, who help to press the point home with practical action – 'If you speak to me

15

like that one more time, you're not going out on your bike.' And this raises the major difficulty of television as a means of linguistic communication: it is only one-way.

Television exposes children to language which can be grammatically rich and complex. Even despised commercials and cartoons can show children interesting vocabulary and ideas which they might not hear of elsewhere. An example, taken completely at random, from turning the television on while typing, is: 'You can't buy a more effective painkiller.' The message here is actually that 'Our product is better at getting rid of pain than all other painkillers which are on sale'. Putting the advertised message in the negative form is presumably intended to have more impact for adult viewers. But negatives are generally harder to grasp than positives and the implied double negative here would almost certainly be misinterpreted by many children. (The two implied negatives are firstly, that you can't buy a certain kind of painkiller; secondly, that there is no painkiller better than this one.) The message might be seen as 'You can't buy a painkiller (of any kind)'. To understand this message, children of pre- and primary school age would probably need quite a lot of adult explanation, which is unlikely to be forthcoming during casual viewing of a commercial break.

Nevertheless, where conscious efforts are made by a supportively viewing adult, language skills can be taught via television. Patricia Marks Greenfield in *Mind and Media* describes how educational television in the African country of Niger was able to teach French to educationally disadvantaged children, who did not speak French. Pictures were used to make the meanings of words clear, and dramatic skits were used to demonstrate dialogue and actions. Allied with active post-viewing discussions with the adult assistant (not a trained teacher), children scored well on tests in all subjects, all given in French. They were also very enthusiastic about the lessons. Thus, the medium can be used in a positive way to facilitate language learning, so long as interested adults facilitate it.

Children have a 'natural' ability to learn and use language, which is observed by all parents, as their child develops from the babbling six-month-old, through the tersely commanding toddler with two-word sentences, to the argumentative four-year-old who can't see why he or she should stop to put a coat on. In our book *Baby Language*, I and two other psychologist colleagues with a special interest in language and communication looked at the very early stages of language development. These stages show how children understand and use many of the rules of language and have many non-verbal means of expressing themselves before they can speak fluently (which most children manage to do between the ages of two and three). When you study the fascinating process of how children learn language, you can see that, despite the thousands of different languages spoken in the world, children everywhere go through broadly similar stages of language development, regardless of their native tongue. They start by labelling, giving familiar things names: *Mummy, Daddy, dog, cup, shoe* and so on. They also pick up other useful single words like 'no'. Then, at around 18 months, they begin to combine words – a crucial stage which shows that they are beginning to understand the relationships between objects and events. A door slamming will produce 'Mummy go?' for example. Very rapidly, during the third and fourth years, the whole basic apparatus of spoken grammar will be acquired: verb tenses, plurals, definite and indefinite articles, possessives and so on. All this will reflect the child's widening knowledge of the world around him; of the relationships in it; of the fact that there is a past, which we can remember and express by saying 'Mummy went' (or 'goed', in the early stages) and a future, which can be expressed by 'when will Mummy go?'

This impressive achievement happens without any formal teaching in nearly all children, including the handicapped and impoverished. It can thus be easy to underestimate the importance of input from other people. Most modern studies of language acquisition now stress the help that children get from the people around them. Parents, for instance, tend to adapt their language so that their children can understand it. This kind of special language, with its short, complete sentences, its frequent repetitions, its regular questions, its references only to things that the child is likely to know from experience, has been called 'Motherese'. The child's acquisition of language is also rooted in everyday experience, as the example of 'if . . . then' constructions given above demonstrates. A child who repeatedly won't eat his or her dinner, or drops toys behind the fridge, soon learns what the consequences will be! Play is the other great teacher about the relationships between objects and events in the world. Play with models, dolls, construction toys, dressing-up clothes, materials like sand, water, mud and stones, and with other children, provides experiences which extend the child's vocabulary. The need to communicate becomes stronger so that the child can express the relationships he or she is discovering.

On the plus side, television can and does offer children a wide variety of language styles and vocabulary, uttered by a wide variety of people, using different accents and figures of speech. By demonstrating actions with pictures, television can underline the meaning of what is going on and make a story clearer. There is evidence that pictures can demonstrate causal processes, such as the growth of a tree from a seed, more effectively than words alone, as a 1976 Swedish study with primary school children showed. Studies from America have shown that children are attentive to the sound and that the soundtrack is important in attracting attention. Even pre-school children can pick up nuances in voices which indicate that something might be going to happen. Nevertheless, although television does appear to provide a great deal of language experience for children, the crucial element of feedback from other people is missing. It is unlikely that young children could learn their own language from television alone. But the fact that children cannot learn language from television alone is not an indictment of television. Children cannot learn to read simply by having books around them either. In both cases, the role of adults in encouraging children's conversational and literary skills is crucial.

The language of film

Of course, there is a sense in which film and television have their own 'language'. The way films and television programmes are made is governed by a consistent set of rules which determine how separate shots are edited together to make a coherent sequence, or a scene, or an episode or a full-length narrative. Techniques such as fades, flashbacks, and cutting from one scene to another are used to indicate time passing, or people moving. Camera movements, such as zooming and panning, direct attention, and suggest different points of view – a camera panning along a scene can create the impression of a person scanning a distant horizon, for instance. Close-up shots convey emphasis, suggest emotion or create tension. As already mentioned, American research carried out by Robin Smith indicates that, at four, some children can understand montage – the juxtaposition of different shots to create an implied connection betweeen the two shots. Four-year-olds can supply the missing details of an event in later reconstructions with toys. However, many young children cannot do this; it is an ability that improves with age.

Close-ups can be particularly confusing; some German research in the 1950s found that six-year-olds who saw a film of the folk tale *Town and Country Mouse* thought that the mouse was a different animal in close-up than in long shot. Some American research in 1981 found that many children thought that bars of chocolate shown in close-up were bigger and more desirable than the same bars shown in a wider shot, which made them appear smaller. The IBA's code of advertising conduct insists that advertisements for toys include other objects next to the toys which give a correct impression of scale; the most commonly used scale reference point is a child's hands. Pre-school programmes, such as the late *Play School*, will do the same thing – particularly if an object could possibly be frightening in a large close-up, filling the screen. One producer said that when they had shown a plum in close-up, some young children she knew had been frightened by it – it looked so huge and menacing!

My own research with close-ups found that adults appeared to be unconsciously influenced by close-ups when recalling events they had seen on television (though children weren't). I showed them short sequences of television material, taken from *Play School*, in which the same actions were shown either in an unbroken middle-distance (mid) shot, or in versions which cut to a close-up of something that the presenter was demonstrating (a toy, an animal, some food, a drawing). These viewers found it very difficult to notice the difference between the two versions, even when I gave them several opportunities to do so, after my experiments were over. They were very sceptical that they had taken part in any kind of experiment at all, as they couldn't see the difference between the two versions until I pointed it out to them.

Nevertheless, these unnoticed differences had significant effects on the way that viewers remembered the events later. After viewing these action sequences for the first time, adult viewers were more likely to remember the object being demonstrated – and to forget who the presenter was – in the close-up versions, than in the ordinary uncut mid-shot versions. In the uncut versions viewers remembered both the presenter and the toy about equally. The close-up seemed to unbalance their memory of the event by its emphasis on the toys and other objects. Five- and six-year-old children were not affected by the close-up in this way. Their memory for the events was the same in both the mid-shot and close-up versions. It's likely that at this age children are still learning about the emphatic functions of techniques like close-up; many children may not realise that a switch to close-up is a 'rule' which determines a way of interpreting the programme-maker's intended 'meaning': the 'meaning' in this case being that 'this object has some special significance – look more closely at it'.

A further interesting outcome of my research was that people were more likely to use passive sentences in recalling the events shown in close-up versions. They did not do this in non-close-up versions. In a passive sentence, the order of an ordinary active sentence is turned around to give more emphasis to the person or thing on the receiving end of an action: 'The mother baths the baby' becomes 'The baby is bathed by the mother' – which gives the baby more prominence, just as close-up does. In my research people were more likely to say things like 'A baby was being bathed by a mother' when they were recalling a close-up version. It seemed, from this – again – unconscious choice of unusual wording (passives are much rarer in normal speech than active sentences are), that linguistic grammar and film/TV 'grammar' have something in common. For adults, the 'grammar' of close-up seemed to be best expressed in the grammatical form of speech of passive sentences. It may be that young children don't fully understand the function of close-ups – just as they find passive sentences difficult to understand or memorise until they are about six or seven.

An interesting study done in 1975 by Uta Frith, a developmental psychologist, and Jocelyn Robson, a film student at London University, also looked at children's understanding of cinematic 'grammar', using children aged seven, nine and 13. Frith and Robson studied what is known as 'directional continuity' in a series of shots in a short film of a boy and his dog. Directional continuity requires the editing of the sequence to follow the movement of the main subject of the action – in this case the dog. The first shot of the four shots in the film showed the dog entering on the left of the frame; then, in the second shot, the dog carried on in the same direction, and bounded up to the boy, who threw a ball back in the direction the dog had come from; then, in the third shot, the dog ran back out of the left of the frame; then, in the fourth shot, the dog re-entered the left of the frame once more to give the ball to the boy. A logical, 'real life' start to the sequence would show the boy throwing the ball first – and many children who were asked to put still pictures of the film in the correct order, showed this – not the dog running into the left of the frame of the first shot.

The authors of the study reversed the second and fourth shot in one version of the film, so that the dog was not consistently entering and re-entering the frame on the left. Children who saw this 'muddled' version, without directional continuity, were significantly less likely to remember the order of events of what they had seen than children who had seen the 'rule-governed' version, which followed the dog's directional continuity. The authors argue that 'even seven-year-olds show sensitivity to standard film rules' and that this sensitivity has something in common with the way children acquire the rules of verbal language. Certainly much less is known about how children acquire film and television 'rules' than about how they acquire language, although some of the studies mentioned above suggest that the two sets of skills are not entirely separable. Given the amount of time young children spend watching television, it would be helpful to know more about this – and about its relationship with language generally. What all these studies do show is that the ability to 'decode' and utilise film and TV grammar improves with age and thus appears to be related to development generally.

Understanding stories

The main form employed by television – certainly by the kind of television that young children like to watch – is the narrative. Dramatised stories, like *Postman Pat* and *Bertha, the Big Machine*, take simple events, like the rescue of a kitten, or a breakdown in Bertha's machinery, and turn

22

them into mini-dramas. To understand even simple stories like these, children must have an ability to understand the underlying logic of events: that when Pat abandons his van, it is because a tree has fallen across the road earlier. Virtually all stories, from *Postman Pat* to *Middlemarch* have the same basic structure: an introductory setting of the scene and an introduction of the main character(s): the posing of a problem or conflict for the main character(s); and the resolution of the conflict. In a complex adult novel like *Middlemarch*, of course, there will be sub-plots and subsidiary characters and any number of stages in the resolution of the problem – nevertheless, the basic structure is the same.

Children obviously learn about cause and effect in events in real life – how problems occur, and how they are resolved. Well before their first birthday, frustrated babies can use their logical abilities to get round obstacles placed in their way by parents seeking to protect either child or home, or both. I once watched a tiny eleven-month-old girl push a heavy coffee table inch by inch towards a shelf on which stood some forbidden biscuits, so that she could stand on the table and reach the biscuits. As a storyline, this event would be: baby and baby's mother are in room (scene-setting); baby's mother removes biscuits from baby (problem); baby invents solution to problem i.e. table-pushing, and uses it to solve problem (resolution). (There was actually a sequel in which mother removed biscuits and put them on an even higher shelf – moral: mothers know best.)

In drama, particularly televised drama, with its cuts from scene to scene, the links between events are not always as obvious as they are in life. Even in a very simple pre-school programme, like *Postman Pat*, there may be an intervening scene, featuring other characters, between the tree falling down and the van being abandoned. If the sequence of events is interrupted, young children may have difficulty in maintaining earlier events in memory, in order to understand later ones. Thus they may be completely baffled by what is going on in the later part of the story.

As with other abilities, there are developmental changes in the way children understand stories. In his book *Children in Front of the Small Screen*, Grant Noble describes research in which children of different ages were asked to remember incidents from televised stories, and to put pictures of scenes from stories in the correct order after seeing a programme. He studied children from five to 13 and, with every year of age, the children's ability to remember incidents and to order them correctly progressively increased. Very young children may see television scenes as a series of separate events, with no connection between them. Noble describes an incident in which he watched an episode of the puppet series *Thunderbirds* with a five-year-old and a six-year-old. At each commercial break, the five-year-old asked: 'Is that the end?' The six-year-old was sufficiently advanced in his understanding of story structure to be able to reply: 'Of course not, stupid, they have not rescued the trapped people yet.' He was able to see that the problem had not yet been resolved, and therefore the story could not be at an end.

Television imposes extra problems in the understanding of story structure, because of its editing techniques; the relationship between cause and effect may be left out and the viewer has to make the inference for him or herself. When Postman Pat is seen driving his van in one shot, and riding a bicycle in a later one, children have to deduce that he has abandoned his van because of the tree across the road and that he has been forced to borrow a bike. Such deductions require a power of logical thinking which very young children, particularly those unfamiliar with stories, do not always have. They are not yet able, in Noble's words, to 'mentally retrace the events seen and . . . to predict forward.' Programmes which demonstrate links between cause and effect, taking place in real time, and showing how things are done without recourse to constant editing (like the BBC's late *Play School*), are more respectful to young children's abilities, than are programmes with frequent, visually dazzling changes of shot and changes of scene.

A programme which is particularly insensitive to young children's limitations in this respect is *Sesame Street*, though it is aimed at the pre-school age range. Grant Noble criticises its attention-getting devices borrowed from TV commercials as 'a whole series of gimmicks . . . such as loud noises, monkeys, bouncy music, other children and repetitive commercial breaks'. He describes how one three-year-old could understand only three out of 36 sequences in the programme, whereas her six-year-old sister could understand 28-30 sequences. Programmes for young children need to be aware of the need to spell things out; parents watching with young children can help to compensate for misunderstandings by doing some spelling out for them. 'What's happened to Postman Pat's van?', for instance. In this way, although there may be age limits on a young child's intellectual abilities, parents can use a television story to help make the most of the abilities the child already has. However, research carried out on *Sesame Street* by Gavriel Salomon in Israel did show that children's understanding and learning from the programme improved the more they got used to it (not just with age – a control group who didn't see the series did not make the same headway). Children also learned more when mothers watched and discussed with them.

Children are limited by the developmental stage they happen to be going through so that, in general, five-year-olds will do less well in memory or comprehension tasks than six-year-olds, and six-year-olds will do less well than seven-year-olds. But with television, as with other activities, there is still scope for improving the understanding and enjoyment of individual children, by identifying their particular difficulties. The mistakes children make can tell us a lot about their thought processes: if commercial breaks seem to be the end of the programme, what is it that gives the five-year-old in Grant Noble's work, mentioned above, this impression? He does at least recognise that there has been an abrupt change of scene from one 'story' to another; he knows that commercials are not part of the programme. How does he know this? What are the particular 'signifiers' of commercials that lead him to believe that the programme has finished? One American study which followed the television-viewing career of three children over a period of years, found the earliest recognition of the difference between programme and commercial at the age of two and a half. Commercials look and sound different from programmes and children notice these differences.

Adults need to be aware of the difficulties that young children might be having, and the mistaken – but still logical – inferences they might be making about television programmes. Programme makers need to improve their understanding of children's mental processes and parents need to keep a check on what their children are gaining, or not, from the programmes that they watch. Far from being mindless, television actually poses problem-solving tasks for children which are not found in other media. It is a particularly rich source of information about stories, and how stories ought to be structured. For instance, the daily serialised story, as in *Jackanory*, or even in *Neighbours*, can teach children how to follow a plot from one episode to another. The very fact of the programme being on every day of the week can help a child to learn when to expect the end and when the story cannot yet have come to an end. Elinor at six, enjoyed the serialisation of Ted Hughes' *The Iron Man* on *Jackanory*, and knew that when the Iron Man got buried in the pit, which she recognised as a classic story climax of the 'baddie' being killed, it still couldn't be the end, 'because it was only Wednesday'. *Jackanory* stories always end on Friday.

Television and social development

Television is often accused of having effects (mainly bad ones) on children's attitudes and relationships – in fact this is seen as its main source of influence, overriding all other influences. Children's earliest and main relationships are with their parents, in particular the mother during babyhood. Even if we no longer accept the Freudian view that what happens in early infancy is of irreversible and paramount importance to the rest of life, it is still clear from all kinds of evidence that the experiences of early childhood can have a profound effect on the sorts of adults people become. Modern theories of developmental psychology now stress, too, the importance of children's relationships with their wider families and friends as they grow up. Children can become very attached to siblings, grandparents, childminders, nannies and friends. Research suggests that these attachments do not interfere with their attachment to their parents – they may well enhance it, particularly if the attachment exists all-round, for example, if a beloved grandmother is also close to the child's parent.

At around the age of three to four children become capable of forming stable friendships with other children and during the primary school years, friends can become the most intense relationships in children's lives, even though mum, dad and siblings still provide important background security. For teenagers, peers are paramount and parents fall from their pedestal and become a source of oppression and lack of understanding, at least some of the time, and for some unfortunate parents, all of the time. This rebellious phase, like the toddler tantrum phase, the waking at night phase, the refusal to eat anything other than bananas and biscuits phase, inevitably passes – particularly when teenagers grow up to become young adults and parents themselves. There are, of course, children who grow up to be criminals and terrorists. There are children, often children who have been badly treated by their own parents, who become very bad parents in their own turn. The roots and causes of such anti-social behaviour are complex. They have always existed and it would be difficult for even the most avid television-hater to blame them exclusively on television.

The main point being made in the present chapter, about children and how they grow up, is that children develop according to a biological 'blueprint', which is very broadly similar for children everywhere. But this pattern unfolds in a social and cultural context, not in isolation, and this will vary from place to place and from time to time. It also varies from child to child, because every child is genetically and experientially unique. Television is part of a whole network of experiences and relationships in children's lives and the way it affects a child interacts with all these other experiences and relationships. Television's impact depends on how the medium is used, or not used, or abused, in the child's family, and it also depends on the individual child and the stage he or she has reached, and the sort of person he or she is. Television is not all-powerful. It can provide examples of some of life's possibilities for children. It can give them ideas for play and satisfy some of their curiosity for knowledge. But it cannot play for them. Similarly, it can show them how other people, including 'bad' people, behave, but it cannot bring them up to be nice or nasty people. Only families and communities can do that.

As critics of television have pointed out, while television can show children what a snake or an eagle looks like, it cannot give them the experience of seeing and holding and caring for a real animal, fascinating though programmes such as the BBC's *The Really Wild Show* may be. These real-life experiences have to be provided by other people. Programmes like this do stimulate an interest in animals, as the thousands of letters they receive show. They also bring an awareness of global issues, such as ecology, into children's lives in ways which they can understand. Urban children, who may not have access to animals, can be encouraged to look into their environments for evidence of wild-life – insects, birds, foxes and so on. Television thus works best in a partnership with other interested adults who can help children to follow up what they have seen and heard in programmes. But critics of television who complain that its experiences are only simulated, and thus not really effective, cannot have it both ways. If the educational experiences of television are not 'real', and have to be reinforced in home or school, why should the social impact of television be any more real? Both intellectually, and socially, television will have most impact when it is reinforced or modified by experiences in the child's own world.

Those who criticise television for turning children into a generation of passive box-watchers could perhaps ask themselves what their own communities are actively doing to provide more enriching experiences for the young, including making them more aware of their environment. How much space, security, freedom, adult attention and time are provided for children and the people who look after them in your neighbourhood? And if there is not enough, what are you doing about it? Information and examples of skills provided by television need to be reinforced by experience if they are to be any use to children, and the same applies to behaviour. The social and behavioural effects of television will be looked at more closely in later chapters. Television exists in an environment, not a vacuum, which is full of social examples and constraints provided by family and community. Children's social and intellectual development is also subject to biological limitations which mean that it can be very difficult for them to either understand or imitate televised examples until they have reached the requisite maturity. By this time, other factors may be operating to ensure that children do not imitate bad examples – for instance, their awareness of the difference between fiction and reality and a desire to conform to the social rules of the people they care about.

Television itself also provides many different examples of human behaviour which can help to create what one researcher, Mallory Wober at the IBA, has called a 'dilution effect'. Television itself has a role to play in the child's world, which will be discussed more fully in Chapter 9 which deals with entertainment. It is unlikely that seeing violence on television can completely override the decency and good manners of a whole household in which such attitudes are consistently valued and practised. It is likewise sadly unlikely that seeing examples of kindness and unselfishness on television can compensate for the painful experiences of a child growing up in a brutal and violent household. As anyone who has studied the history of childhood knows, brutal and violent households have always existed and did not need television to bring them into existence. Both intellectually and socially, the child is likely to learn best from television if it is integrated with and related to other areas of his life. This means not banning television, nor blaming it, but using it.

3 | The other side of the partnership: television

If defining a child is difficult, it can be equally difficult to define 'television'. What is television? From a child's point of view, it is part of the furniture – a 'box in the corner', to use Gwen Dunn's phrase from her book of this name. This box almost magically transmits images, sounds, stories and information to the child, and brings people into the living room with whom he or she soon becomes familiar. The television set, and the people it reveals, are part of the family. As such, television can be defined as an intensely personal, small-scale domestic phenomenon. Paradoxically, however, it is also a vast, global, multi-billion pound industry. Television reaches audiences of millions, and the success of a programme will be judged, not on its relationship with individuals, but primarily on how big an audience it attracts. Children's programmes, some of which attract audiences of less than a million (very small in audience research terms) can thus be vulnerable in any broadcasting system which primarily depends on large audiences to attract money, either from advertising or from other sources. As Clare Mulholland, Deputy Director of Television at the IBA, put it:

> There have to be loss leaders in children's programmes in advertising terms: cartoons are popular, but we also see our role as taking children from easy viewing to something more stimulating. Children's programmes must contain information and education too.

Nevertheless, even in size terms, 'minority' television reaches audiences which, for other media, would be considered

31

wonderful. On one day in January 1988, for instance, ITV's *Rainbow* achieved an audience of about 549,000 four- to nine-year-olds. A touring theatre company would feel very gratified if it managed to attract even a quarter of that number during its tour, and a readership this size for a book would give it massive best-seller status. Thus, although television, through its position in the living room, enjoys a very intimate relationship with individuals, the huge numbers of individuals involved mean that decisions have to be made on a much larger national and international scale. This inevitably means that, for some individuals, and perhaps sometimes for all, their relationship with the box in the corner is occasionally disappointing. The most powerless individuals, like children, may end up being the most frequently disappointed; on Budget Day in 1988, ITV's children's programmes were taken off the air altogether. On the same day, Channel 4's management board endorsed Michael Grade's decision to bring C4's children's programmes to an end.

Television's output

In this country it is possible for a child to turn on the television at almost any time of the day or night and see something. The availability of programmes will increase when mass satellite broadcasting begins later this year. At the moment, most of television's output comes from the two main broadcasting organisations, the BBC (British Broadcasting Corporation) and ITV (Independent Television) which is regulated by the IBA (though this will be abolished under planned Government legislation and replaced by the Independent Television Commission which will have less control). Between them, they provide about 300 hours of television a week. Particularly within the independent commercial system, programmes are likely to vary from region to region: ITV has 15 regional companies, with the Big Five – Central (based in Nottingham), Granada (based in Manchester), London Weekend, Thames and Yorkshire – providing most of the output that goes on the air nationally. In addition, there is Channel 4, also the responsibility of the IBA, which is committed to making programmes 'appealing to tastes and interests not generally catered for by ITV' (to quote the *IBA Yearbook* for 1988) – though not, as we have seen, now including children. There are also a number of cable and satellite companies which reach much smaller audiences at the moment, although it is assumed that this will change under the new deregulated broadcasting conditions. Under these conditions, people will have the 'choice' of buying satellite receivers in addition to their licence fees. Children's Channel is an example of a satellite TV company, which specialises in catering for a minority audience. An increasing number of programmes (a quota of 25 per cent has been agreed on between the broadcasting organisations and the government) are being made by independent producers – the equivalent of small broadcasting businesses – and sold to the main broadcasting networks. A proportion of programmes transmitted in this country come from other countries: USA, Australia, Canada and Europe.

Between them, the broadcasting companies provide programmes on a wide variety of topics: there is light entertainment, drama, soap opera, sport, news and current affairs, documentaries, educational programmes for adults and children, music, dance, chat shows, films, children's programmes. Services aimed directly at particular sections of the audience, such as weather forecasting, the Open University, *Crimewatch* and teletext, are provided too. Recently there has been an increasing number of 'access' programmes, such as Channel 4's *The Right to Reply* and the BBC's *Open Air* in which viewers get the chance to appear in front of the camera and to give their points of view. Children's programmes, such as *Going Live, Take Two* and *Newsround Extra*, frequently feature children making comments about programmes, music or current affairs. All this helps to create an impression of dialogue between the programme makers and the audience.

Nevertheless, despite its apparent naturalism and intimacy when viewed from the living room, television behind the scenes is a cumbersome and artificial medium, requiring a mass of technical equipment for sound, lighting and staging while recording programmes, and further elaborate techniques for editing and transmitting them. In this sense, it is a very unnaturalistic medium, in which even realistic-looking events, such as a family mealtime, have to be rehearsed and re-shot, to convey a plausible impression of the real thing. The techniques that TV uses for 'short-cutting' time and space, by cutting from one scene to another, distance the tidiness of an edited programme from the messy chaos of real experience even further. This is something that children have to learn if they are to come to terms with television, and to understand it properly. Life does not occur in short scenes, with carefully staged climaxes before commercial breaks, as it does on TV.

Children's television

Within the main output, the BBC provides around 16 hours a week of programmes especially for children, and the independent companies around 11 hours a week. There is also an increasing video market of children's programmes, which mean that children can watch tapes of *Thomas the Tank Engine* or *Postman Pat* whenever they like, parents' sanity permitting. Children's Channel, on satellite, provides around four hours a day of programmes entirely for children, to around 140,000 homes in this country and more in other countries. The aim of children's programming, according to Anna Home, Head of the Children's Department at the BBC, is:

To provide a microcosm of adult television for the children's audience, ranging from drama to news, and including light entertainment, information, magazines, documentaries, story-telling, plus specialised programmes for the very young child.

The aim of the various ITV companies – not co-ordinated into one department, as at the BBC, but with their own Children's Sub-Group – is similar: Clare Mulholland describes their priority as 'variety – a range of programmes across the week'. This means trying to cater for all ages of children, for different types of children and to provide 'information as well as entertainment'. Children's programmes on both BBC and ITV have their own precious 'blocks' of airtime – primarily after school, between about 4pm and 5.30pm. Programmes for pre-schoolers are transmitted mid-morning and post-lunch (around 1.30pm) and are usually short – 20 minutes maximum. There are also Saturday morning magazine programmes, such as *Going Live* and Sunday cartoons and teatime serials.

In this country, we have become so used to special TV provision for children, with its own special times, reaching back to *Muffin the Mule* and *The Flowerpot Men* in the 1950s, that it can be startling to realise that such provision is not taken for granted everywhere, particularly not in the USA. There, an organisation called Action for Children's Television (ACT) campaigns against the general lack of provision for children's programmes, and the takeover of what children's airtime there is by toy-based cartoons: there are now more than 45 programmes based on toys being shown in America. *Thundercats* is an example which found its way over here. Many original programmes have later spin-offs into the toy market, but what's happening in the US is that the toy comes first and the programme is created to help sell it. ACT's objection is not only to the commercial exploitation of children, but also to the driving out of the sort of high-quality programmes, such as drama and news, that we take for granted here. A concern that similar indifference to children's needs might develop in the UK as broadcasting becomes more and more deregulated and subject purely to market forces, has led to the formation of a British equivalent of ACT – British Action for Children's Television (BACTV).

Anna Home, Head of BBC Children's Department, defends children's television as providing something that adult television cannot and she rejects the idea that childhood is a Victorian cultural invention (see Chapter 4): 'Children's television addresses its audience specifically and in its own terms . . . It can present children with their own literature, music and art and reflect their interests and enthusiasms as well as worries and concerns.' She points out that in many parts of Europe and America:

> Children's television has been blended into family viewing, thus depriving children of something that is really theirs. A wish to grow up is very strong in our society, but childhood is valuable, and children's television should be part of childhood.

The note of social concern and responsibility for the welfare of children struck here is echoed by Lewis Rudd, Controller of Young People's Television at Central TV, who has presided over some of the more controversial outputs of children's television, such as *A Couple of Charlies*, a drama serial about child abuse:

> Such programmes set out to provoke thought or action. A drama series can discuss issues which children want to talk about and show children who might be in this situation that there is something they can do to get themselves out of it.

Central worked very closely with the National Society for the Prevention of Cruelty to Children (NSPCC) in preparing this series and in dealing with the responses to it. Rudd went so far as to tell his staff: 'If the NSPCC don't think this film is positively helpful, it won't go out.' It did go out – and to the protests from some adults who complained that their six-year-olds found it disturbing, Rudd's reply was: 'Upsetting a six-year-old in a secure home is not as important as giving help and guidance to kids in this situation.' Children's programme makers thus seem to be prepared to go out on a moral limb to an extent not required of adult producers – *Grange Hill* and its treatment of drugs, bullying and petty crime is another example – to fulfil what they see as a serious responsibility to their audience.

This responsibility is also reflected in the internal guidelines used by both BBC and ITV to help producers decide what is and is not acceptable in programmes likely to be seen by children. For instance, the IBA advises against bad language; blasphemy; dangerous examples such as hanging, playing with plastic bags or abandoned fridges; it advises special care in scenes which involve 'violence, menace and threats', especially in domestic settings. It is also opposed to motivations based on greed and luck in programmes – especially those which involve prizes. Both the main broadcasting authorities follow a 'watershed' policy, whereby programmes which might be disturbing to children are shown after 9pm. After this time, the policy is, to quote the IBA guidelines: 'Parents may reasonably be expected to share responsibility for what their children see.' These are some of the attitudes of the producers of the television service towards children. What is children's response to them?

The child audience

Trying to determine what children watch and when is a complicated business. Statistics suggesting that all children watch 20 to 30 hours a week, or spend more time in front of the TV than they do at school, are common currency, but it is difficult to find a factual, or properly researched, basis for them. One of the problems in finding out how many hours particular groups of children, or individuals, watch is that the main research figures regularly collected about audiences aren't measured in this way. When you read that

Neighbours got an audience of 15 million and later on in the evening *EastEnders* got an audience of 13 million, the bald audience figures can't tell us how many of these two groups of millions were the same people. It is likely that quite a few of the *Neighbours* audience also watched *EastEnders*; it's also possible that many people watching *EastEnders* hadn't seen *Neighbours* perhaps because they were not home from work in time. To know how many hours a day, on average, a child watches television, it is necessary to track him or her as an individual right through the evening for several weeks, noting what he or she is watching and not watching. To know how many hours a representative sample of thousands of children watches television, it would be necessary to do the same for all these thousands of individuals – a mammoth task, but certainly worth doing in order to establish some reliable estimates of how many hours children *really* spend TV-viewing. In the meantime, what we have are only rough estimates.

Both the BBC and ITV subscribe to the Broadcasters' Audience Research Board (BARB) which gives them information gathered by the research organisation AGB (Audits of Great Britain) about what audiences watch around the country. There are about 8.7 million children between four and 15, which constitutes about 17 per cent of the population. Two thirds of households at any given moment have no children (although, obviously, which households these are are constantly changing, as older children leave home and new ones are born). At any single point in time, therefore, families are a minority audience, and this fact is sometimes used by programme makers to justify playing down the child's point of view. Nevertheless, put another way, every member of the audience has been a child, and, in this sense, the welfare of children concerns 100 per cent of the population, because childhood experiences can profoundly affect the sort of adults people become.

BARB obtains its audience estimates from a panel of around 8,000 households around the country, which includes representatives of all social classes and age groups. From their viewing patterns, estimates of the whole audience in each group – for instance four- to nine-year-olds, or male adults – can be extrapolated to the nearest thousand. This is how the 549,000 audience for *Rainbow* mentioned above was arrived at. The BARB audience figures only begin with four-year-olds – so reasonably accurate estimates for a very important group of child viewers (the under-fours) remain unobtainable. We should thus be cautious about believing claims that pre-school children watch over 20 hours of television; nobody really knows what *all* pre-school children watch. Figures for what children like (Appreciation Indexes) are also collected by BARB, for the benefit of the pro-gramme makers who have to pay for the information. These are confidential.

Both the BBC and the IBA have their own research departments which can provide more detailed information about particular programmes and particular audiences, as well as about particular issues, like violence, or the impact of the AIDS campaign. Much of this research is for the benefit of the broadcasting organisations themselves. It is not always made available to the interested public, unless it is on a burning issue like violence. There is very little research on children and television carried out in academic institutions in this country – unlike the USA, which, although it falls short of the UK in the quality of its children's programmes, produces some excellent academic research on children and television, some of it quoted in this book. Advertisers carry out a great deal of market research on audiences which is oriented towards trying to sell children things and is thus, inevitably, somewhat slanted. Sometimes schools will carry out their own small-scale projects or surveys on what children watch.

Programme makers rely heavily on the letters and phone calls they receive to tell them what their viewers think. Such information, however, is likely to be unrepresentative of the population as a whole; letter writers are a special kind of enthusiastic person. Also, according to Roy Thompson, Deputy Head of the BBC Children's Department, children are more likely to write in praise of something, adults to complain. The contrary view from either group is thus less likely to get heard. In general, therefore, the overall picture of what children watch what programmes, and when, and why – let alone what they get out of these programmes – is still a patchy one. This is why we should always be cautious when we read bold claims in the popular press that children watch television all the time, or that they are adversely affected by certain kinds of programme. We need to be equally cautious about claims made by programme makers that their programmes got an overwhelming response from viewers. Such claims are likely to be based on limited evidence.

What children do watch

The viewing figures collected by BARB/AGB enable us to get an idea of how large the proportion of children in the audience for different programmes is. (Children are defined as people between the ages of four and 15.) Programme makers themselves are able to subdivide the child audience further into four- to nine-year-olds or ten- to 16-year-olds. The AI (Appreciation Index) figures, which are confidential, can be further subdivided into age groups of four plus, seven plus and ten plus, but the public never get to see these AI figures, so it is difficult to know in any detail what younger or older children watch and enjoy.

The first point to make about viewing figures is that they vary according to all sorts of factors, such as one-off showings of popular films like *Carry on Cruising*, which got into the Top Ten programmes watched by children in August 1987, or by big events like royal weddings. Inevitably, what children watch is affected by the other things they have to do in their lives. The BBC carried out an enormously detailed survey in 1983/84, called *Daily Life in the 1980s* in which 6,000 individuals aged four and over were interviewed over several days, in both winter and summer. How these individuals spent their time was broken down into a 'time band analysis' in which the day was divided into 15- or 30-minute segments, starting at 6am and ending at 2.30am the next morning, and people were asked to say what they were doing at each time. There were three categories of children: 4 to 7s, 8 to 11s and 12 to 15s. The sorts of things mentioned included being at home; being at work/school; being asleep; gardening; sport; childcare; shopping; talking; wandering around (an activity mentioned by several under-nines, but hardly any 12 to 15s!); hobbies, games and playing; and of course, watching television.

This analysis reveals that for most of the 24 hours most children are not watching television. When they do watch, they watch much more in winter than they do in summer. Winter viewing figures during the day and early evening are virtually halved during the summer; for example, 74 per cent of 4 to 7s were watching TV at 4pm on winter weekdays, the start of children's programmes. Only 37 per cent were watching at this time in the summer. However, as might be expected on lighter evenings, slightly more children are watching later at night in the summer: 8 per cent of 8 to 11s in this survey were watching TV at 10pm in the winter, 11 per cent were watching in the summer. Eighty-eight per cent of this age group were asleep at this time in the winter, as might be expected, and a further 7 per cent were in bed, but not asleep (a problem with which many parents are familiar). These figures belie the view that most British parents allow their young children to stay up till all hours watching unsuitable movies. This survey provides no evidence for such a view.

The survey also reveals that the biggest concentration of the child audience occurs in the 4 to 7 age group – 78 per cent of them are watching TV at 4.30pm (the highest reported percentage for children's TV watching in this

41

survey); 65 per cent of 8 to 11s are watching at 4.30 (the highest percentage for this group) and 52 per cent of 12 to 15s. The largest proportion of 12 to 15s watches TV later on – 61 per cent of them between 8.30 and 9.30pm. The popularity of TV viewing is obviously going to decline as children become older and more independent and find other things to do: for example, 8 per cent of 12 to 15s were 'doing sports' at 7pm in the winter, 3 per cent of 8 to 11s were, and no 4 to 7s were. The other most frequently mentioned activities for all children were hobbies/games/playing (even at the peak TV time of 4.30pm, 36 per cent of 4 to 7s were playing), and talking – 20 per cent of 4 to 7s said they were 'talking' at this time. Twelve- to 15-year-olds seem to talk fairly consistently throughout the evening with a peak of 31 per cent at 9pm!

Obviously, children do not do all these things entirely separately. It is likely that they sometimes talk, play and eat at the same time as watching television, and that the combination of activities also depends on what the rest of the family is doing. (Peter Collett's Oxford study of families being filmed as they watched television, recounted in Jane Root's book *Open the Box*, provides fascinating evidence of this.) Indoor activities obviously predominate in the winter; in the summer, the majority of children are not watching television even at peak times. Analyses carried out by the IBA in 1986, when children were asked to keep viewing diaries, found some interesting further subdivisions: for instance, that children from four to 12 watch an average of around five programmes per day; that children between seven and nine are the heaviest viewers; that the older the child, the more likely he or she is to prefer BBC to ITV; that more boys than girls prefer BBC to ITV; that children in socio-economic classes D and E watch most television.

Surveys like these reveal a flexibility in children's television watching, arising from age, class, sex, availability of alternative activities, time of year and time of day. And yet, revealing though they are, these are crude estimates of children's viewing behaviour. They tell us nothing about actual choices in TV watching – for example, which programmes children choose to watch, and why, and why children don't choose to watch certain programmes – nor about how children respond to what they watch. The BARB figures collected each week give a little more insight into children's tastes and choices, and we shall now look at these.

Children's favourite programmes

The children's programme most consistently favoured by children, whenever it is on, (in terms of viewing figures) is *Grange Hill*, BBC1's twice-weekly school drama. Both original showings and repeats regularly top the children's programme weekly Top Ten. It usually gets about 31 to 37 per cent of the audience of 4 to 15s. When the weekly Top Ten of all programmes (including adult ones) watched by children is estimated, *Grange Hill* is only toppled into second place by the universally popular soaps such as *EastEnders* and *Neighbours* (which probably reflects whole family viewing) and then not every time. The reasons for the popularity of *Grange Hill* are discussed more fully in the next chapter. However, for those who think that children watch too much television indiscriminately, it is worth noting that, even allowing for a percentage of children watching ITV, more than half the child audience is not watching this most popular of programmes whenever it is on. Around 40 per cent of the whole child audience is about the highest audience figure that any programme, whether adults' or children's, can hope to get. Again, these viewing figures go well down in the summer, with, for instance, the top programme in the first week of July 1987, *Mysterious Cities of Gold*, having only 25 per cent of the child audience.

Programmes such as BBC1's *Hartbeat*, which demonstrate innovative ways with artistic materials and techniques, are consistently in the Top Ten, and occasionally come first, even where there are cartoons at the same time on the other channel – and cartoons are a major attraction. *Scooby Doo* on ITV, for instance, is sometimes rated even more highly than *Grange Hill*. Factual programmes like *Newsround* and *Blue Peter*, too, are consistently in the Top Ten. Usually, at least half the programmes in the 'universal' Top Ten, that is all programmes watched by children, are children's programmes. Of adult programmes, the top child viewing figures go to programmes such as *EastEnders, Neighbours, Top of the Pops, Bread* and *Blind Date*. Among children's programmes, BBC shows seem to be universally preferred to ITV. Among programmes as a whole, ITV is more frequently represented.

The viewing figures represent only numbers in the audience, not individual responses; nevertheless, even just looking at numbers, it can be seen that children are a discriminating audience and that they very much appreciate having their own programmes. The programmes they most like are not easy viewing – they are drama, stimulating informative shows like *Hartbeat*, comedy, and series which give insight into adult behaviour like *EastEnders* and *Blind Date*.

The IBA study of children's viewing diaries mentioned above found some differences in children's tastes according to programme-type, age and sex. By analysing all the different types of programme children saw, the author of the study worked out that action adventure programmes (the kind with violence in them) accounted for only a small part of children's viewing. The author points out that 'if every film and action adventure title children saw, on average, was violence-loaded, this might amount to only just over four items a week per child, or 11 per cent of their viewing'. He makes the point that the diversity and range of children's viewing is a protective factor against possible harmful effects and serves to 'dilute' them – an important argument for keeping the range of programmes available to children as wide as possible, rather than narrowing it by reducing the number of children's programme outlets available. The most heavily viewed programmes by children in this study were comedy and light entertainment, but 18 per cent of their weekly viewing was accounted for by informative programmes, such as news and magazine programmes. Boys watched more adventure and sport, girls more soap operas. After the age of nine, the proportion of adult programmes watched by children went up.

By looking at some of the bald facts and figures about children's relationship with television, it is possible to see that this relationship is not simple and unified. It varies according to all sorts of factors – the age of the child, what programmes are available, what time of year it is, what time of day it is, what sex he or she is, what class he or she is and what else there is to do. There are more detailed and interesting questions to ask about how children respond to television, what they think of it, what they learn from it, how they use it in their work and play. This will be the subject matter of later chapters in the book. But first, it may be enlightening to look at some of the arguments that have been advanced against television as a medium of entertainment and learning which large numbers of children use and obviously enjoy.

4 | Television – corrupter of the young?

In the fifth century BC Plato devised an ideal state – the Republic – where poetry would be banned. The justification for this was that the great poets like Homer showed people, and even gods, behaving badly, and this set a bad example to the young. According to Plato, 'A child cannot distinguish the allegorical sense from the literal, and the ideas he takes in at that age are likely to become indelibly fixed; hence the great importance of seeing the first stories he hears shall be designed to produce the best possible effect on his character.'

Ever since – from the Catholic Church denouncing the translators of the Bible in the late Middle Ages, through Cromwell and his followers denouncing and closing the theatres, through Richard Steele despising the novel (and Jane Austen stoutly defending it), through the attacks on Hollywood made when film first became a popular medium – eminent voices have been raised denouncing the corrupting effect of the new medium on the vulnerable masses, to whom dangerous knowledge and experience, once the exclusive province of the educated elite, would now become available.

As would be expected, television, as the latest popular medium, now has its denouncers, while the popular media of the past, like the novel and film, are safe to be claimed by the educated classes as 'culture'. Because television is a domestic medium, viewed in the home, it is accused not just of corrupting the less educated, but also of destroying and corrupting generations of children in an unprecedented way.

There are, very broadly, two schools of thought in the many attacks on television purporting to be made on children's behalf. The first is what might be called the 'cultural pessimism' view. Television is considered to be bad because it reduces standards of literacy, artistic appreciation and other expressions of cultural excellence. This view argues that television wreaks its harm by attacking the values of civilised society which are embodied primarily in literary culture. The second school of thought can be summarised as the 'television is bad for your health' approach. This views television as a kind of disease which attacks individuals, rather than society, through damaging their brain cells, or their nervous systems, or their bodies generally. The effect of this disease is to make children passive, hyperactive, violent, overweight, moronic and anti-social. Either way, television is held to be responsible for a new barbarism which, almost single-handedly, is threatening civilisation as we know it. This chapter will look critically at two major representatives of these differing views.

A leading proponent of the cultural pessimism view is Neil Postman. In his much-acclaimed book *The Disappearance of Childhood*, first published in 1982, he is quite explicit as to why television is a bad thing: thanks to the invention of electronic communication, the flow of information about the adult world can no longer be controlled and will become accessible to the young. Postman's argument is that, because information in print is harder to gain access to and involves learning to read, children in the past (at least since the invention of printing) were protected from knowledge about adult behaviour which is assumed to be bad for them. He argues that printing made 'childhood' possible, because it made adult information and skills too difficult for children to obtain, until they had the requisite literacy, which, without any scientific or logical foundation, Postman equates with maturity. Now that print is not the dominant medium, we are reverting to the situation that apparently obtained in the Middle Ages when there was no such thing as childhood.

The assertion that medieval people had no concept of childhood would come as a surprise to the 15th century author of the Brome mystery play *Abraham and Isaac*, and no doubt to his audience, who surely found Abraham's impassioned farewell to his 'dear child' – 'In all thy life thou never grieved me once' – as moving as we find it. But Postman's definition of childhood is not based on emotional universals, but on the curious view that childhood can only exist when knowledge of adult behaviour is restricted.

It is obviously sensible to protect children from information that might cause them distress and harm and it is certainly true that television makes information more pervasive than previous media did. This is why television authorities in this country (to a greater extent than in the USA) have, so far at least, strict guidelines about the sorts of programmes that can be shown while children are most likely to be watching. What causes children distress can be difficult to define and a consensus needs to be reached, based on the wisdom and expertise of people who have the interests of children, including their need for knowledge, at heart. The idea that adult knowledge per se should be kept from children is barely defensible, and seems to rest on the dubious Platonic argument that knowledge is the prerogative of the ruling group in the Republic and can only be made accessible on their say-so. Such an argument allows children no choice in what knowledge they have access to, no possibility of appeal against adult decisions, no matter how arbitrary and unhealthy these decisions are. In fact, it could be argued that children's claim to gain access to knowledge denied to them by adults is one of the defining characteristics of Postman's cultural golden age of childhood, the Victorian and Edwardian periods.

During this period, a number of books for and about children appeared which actively challenged adults' right to keep knowledge from the young. One of my most treasured possessions from my own childhood is an anthology of 19th century children's stories called *Victorian Tales for Girls*, edited by Marghanita Laski and published in 1947. It was given to me for Christmas 1952, just before I was eight. I was an excellent reader and was able to decipher the texts with ease. But, in contradiction to Neil Postman's theory that literacy enables the introduction of adult knowledge to be delayed until children are ready for it, I found many of the ideas and references in the stories strange, alien and sometimes disturbing. Similarly, it will take a young child like my eight-year-old daughter many years to appreciate fully the events and production nuances of *Gone with the Wind*, a film she loves to watch again and again on video. Literacy and maturity are very far from being the same thing, either for books or for television.

In many of the Victorian tales for girls, written between 1860 and 1898, the author uses a plot device – such as running away from an unpopular governess, parents going abroad or children being sent abroad themselves – to get their protected middle-class heroines and heroes away from their comfortable homes and into realms of forbidden experience and knowledge. These children are transplanted into worlds their readers almost certainly know nothing about, but which the authors feel they should know something about. For example, in *The Runaways and the Gypsies* (Anonymous, 1860) aristocratic Bertram and Grace Astley are exposed to the horrors of poverty, cruelty and social ostracism suffered by gypsy travellers on the road. In *The Carved Lions* (Mrs Molesworth, 1895), Geraldine, the heroine, (like her prototype in adult literature, Jane Eyre) suffers the privations of a badly run boarding school. In my favourite story, *The Gate of the Giant Scissors* (Annie Fellows-Johnston, 1898), a little American girl, Joyce, is transplanted to provincial France where she helps to restore a brutally treated goatherd (and realistic details of this brutality are not spared) to his rightful place as grandson of a rich landowner – another classic plot device.

Other authors, such as Edith Nesbit, use magic to transport their children into scenes that adult prohibitions would otherwise prevent them from visiting – as in *Five Children and It* (1902) and *The Phoenix and the Carpet* (1904). In *The Railway Children* (1906), realism is substituted for magic: when their father is imprisoned, Bobbie, Peter, Phyllis and their mother go to live as a one-parent family in a country cottage and, admittedly somewhat patronisingly, have to 'play at being poor for a while'.

Sometimes the cultural transplant is the other way, from poor to rich. In the underestimated and unjustly mocked *Little Lord Fauntleroy* (1886), Frances Hodgson Burnett uses a clever device, transplanting a forthright urban American child, with strongly Republican loyalties, into an English ducal household where, despite heavy doses of sentimentality, he manages to make some pretty outspoken comments on the irrationalities and injustices of the English class system.

Of course, as in traditional stories, these tales for children have to end with the restoration of the hero or heroine to their rightful position in 'the castle', either coming into their inheritance, or being restored to their families. The status quo, having been temporarily disrupted, has to be upheld to ensure the happy, just and reassuring ending required by the young. The transparent plot devices used to bring about these restorations can make such stories very unsatisfactory for adults. However, in one of the very best of children's stories ever written, dating from this period and also written by Frances Hodgson Burnett, artificial upheavals and forced happy endings are eschewed. Apart from the description of the bereavement which brings the heroine from India to England at the beginning of the book, the story of *The Secret Garden* (1911) is set almost entirely in the house and garden of Misselthwaite Manor on the Yorkshire moors. The main events of the plot are generated by the psychological developments taking place in and between the two main child protagonists. Anyone who thinks that the interests of children are better served by keeping them in ignorance of 'adult' emotional and physical truths should read *The Secret Garden* carefully and have another think.

In *The Secret Garden* the boy Colin remains an invalid in bed because he is denied access to the adult knowledge that there is nothing really wrong with him. It is a child, his forthright cousin Mary Lennox, who announces that his paralysis is 'only hysterics' and that he ought to get out of bed and into the open air. The author contrasts the closed house, with its adult conspiracy of silence, fostering sickness and neurosis in children, with the openness of the garden and the moor, where the children are exposed to the 'secrets' of natural growth and regeneration and become healthy and happy. The secrecy of Colin's father, who cannot bear to tell his son the truth about his mother's death and in shunning the truth, also shuns the boy, is contrasted with the openness of working-class Dickon's mother with her 12 children and her trust in and reliance on her oldest son. There are no secrets between Dickon and his mother: 'When she had a spare moment, she liked to go out and talk to him.' Dickon's mother was allowed to come into the secret of the garden: 'It was not doubted that she was "safe for sure".'

This tradition of children's efforts to open up 'secrets' unjustifiably kept from them by adults continues in children's literature to the present day and, predictably, Professor Postman disapproves of it. He has stern words for the novelist Judy Blume, one of the first writers to write truthfully about being an adolescent. Television programmes, too, such as *Grange Hill*, continue to stake out a culture of childhood in which children, not adults, are shown as gaining access to and control over knowledge. No wonder Professor Postman disapproves of television. Nevertheless, it can be argued that the culture of childhood is better defended by guaranteeing children the right to challenge the adult information monopoly, than by saying that childhood consists primarily in information control by adults.

The reality of childhood

In his almost exclusive reliance on academic sources of information about childhood, Postman seems to under-estimate the fact that children have always had plenty of non-literary sources of information about adult behaviour, such as older siblings, or eavesdropping through pub walls (as described by the highly literary rural child Flora Thompson in *Lark Rise to Candleford*). Postman argues that the invention of the telegraph has changed 'the character of information from the personal and regional to the impersonal and global . . . the telegraph began the process of making information uncontrollable'. He quotes with approval the remark of Thoreau who, on hearing that a man in Maine could now send a message by telegraph to a man in Texas, asked, 'But what could they have to say to each other?' Postman sees nothing patronising in this remark, and its snobbish unstated assumption that hicks in Maine and cowpokes in Texas are so limited by their respective environments that they could not possibly have anything in common to talk about. The idea that people in Maine could actually have something to say to people in Texas – or that children in Ethiopia might have something to say to more fortunate children in Britain through a programme like *Blue Peter* – is not considered to be worth defending in Professor Postman's thesis.

In Postman's view, childhood does not consist in anything intrinsic to the state of being a child; it consists solely in a cultural situation, brought about by the invention of print-ing, 'in which a particular form of information, exclusively controlled by adults, was made available in stages to child-ren in what was judged to be psychologically assimilable ways'. Now that print is no longer the dominant medium of information, Postman argues that childhood is coming to an end. To anyone concerned with the actual physical, social and emotional needs of children, as distinct from abstract cultural definitions of childhood, such a view has to be seen as dangerous. Childhood exists as a biological fact – a long period of culturally invariate growth, change and development between birth and puberty – however adults choose to define, or ignore, it. Professor Postman's extraordinarily arbitrary definitions, such as 'We take the word children to mean a special class of people somewhere between the ages of seven, say, and seventeen', betray an alarming unawareness of what being a child actually is. He writes, in italics for special emphasis, that seven 'is the age at which children have command over speech'; if he were acquainted with studies of language acquisition carried out over the last 20 years (contained in, for example, *Early Language* by Peter and Jill de Villiers) he would be aware that command over speech is achieved by most children by around the age of four, and by some as early as two.

Some of the Professor's statements border on absurdity, for instance, his authoritative pronouncements on the fashion industry. 'For all practical purposes,' he wrote in 1982, ' "children's clothing" has disappeared.' Yet children's clothes, although drawing some of their inspiration from adult designs, as always, continue, as they were in 1982, to be dominated by practicality and, above all, washability. One is tempted to ask, when did this man last go shopping? The point here is that, in being so out of touch with the realities of children's lives, Professor Postman is ignoring the very real and important issues raised, not only by the role of television, but by children's never-changing needs for proper nurture and supervision. Children will go on being children, whether Professor Postman thinks there is such a thing as childhood, or not. They will go on being smaller, weaker, less mature and experienced than adults, whether there is television or not.

Children at all times, whether they grew up in the Middle Ages or in the 1980s, have needs which do not change. Young children in the crucially important, but overlooked by Postman, period from birth to seven need continuous nurture simply in order to survive, never mind develop to the best of their potential. A human baby can need feeding up to 14 times in 24 hours during the early weeks of life. It will be six months before solid food can be taken and nearly a year before the baby can feed him or herself with any degree of competence. The child will be around 15 months before he or she can walk, and then not terribly well, and around two and a half before he or she can run; until then, too, frequent cleaning will be required since toilet training is not often possible before then. Children cannot safely find their way around until they are at least five, and in modern cities, probably not until they are nine or ten. Children up to puberty need constant supervision and generate considerable amounts of physical labour in terms of feeding, clothing, keeping clean and transporting. And children, by simple virtue of being children, always did.

The problem with the cultural history of childhood is that it is not written by the people who perform this labour. They were almost certainly far too busy. And, since they were women, even during the great age of literacy ushered in by the Renaissance and praised by Professor Postman, they were denied the educational means to be able to write about it, with one or two heartwarming exceptions, such as Elizabeth Gaskell, novelist and mother of six. Thanks partly to the growth of the electronic media and the loosening of control of the flow of information, many women with dependent children can at last gain access to the 'culture' valued so highly by the Professor and the dozens of male authorities he quotes: they can, for instance, be Open University students. When mothers are actually consulted about children's televiewing habits, they tend to be positive about them, as a study carried out by Cathy Murphy in Nottingham in 1983 showed – more of this in Chapter 5. A survey carried out by the IBA in 1988 (*Violence on Television – What the Viewers Think*) showed that the vast majority of parents do not disapprove of their children watching cartoons or action adventure programmes such as *The A Team*. Are parents, the people who do all the feeding, washing and supervising, right? Or are the academic historians of childhood right? Perhaps the voices of children can add something to the debate . . .

Setting a bad example

In March 1979, an irate *Radio Times* reader wrote in response to the first series of BBC1's *Grange Hill*, a series about a comprehensive school which showed children bullying each other and being cheeky to their teachers: 'Realism is an addictive as well as a heady intoxicant in the sense that the more one has, the more one wants . . . It is unlikely that an entire child viewing audience would be content in meekly watching their TV screens without later trying out this behaviour for themselves.' This argument, so far apart in time from Plato's and yet so similar, rests, like his, on some questionable assumptions: first, that children are passive, sitting 'meekly', imbibing ideas which will become 'indelibly fixed', without any criticism or resistance. Second, that children cannot 'distinguish the allegorical sense from the literal', or the 'realistic' from the real. Third, that seeing or hearing 'good' stories will make children behave in ways acceptable to adult society (although not necessarily appropriate to childhood), and that 'bad' stories will have the opposite effect.

On the first point, as noted in Chapter 2, children are neither meek, nor passive, nor uncritical. What they absorb from television or any other medium may be limited by age or inexperience or modified by viewing with other people. They also have their own discriminatory abilities. Studies with children as young as two, carried out by Daniel Anderson and Elizabeth Lorch in 1983, have shown that they learn to pay attention to 'salient' aspects of television, such as changes of scene, or of sound, because they know these signal that something will happen, and they can also choose to ignore less essential pieces of information.

On the second point, there is ample evidence that even pre-school children know the difference between a story and real life, between a picture and the object shown in it, that 'magic' is something that is only 'pretend' and that pretending to be a mummy or a daddy in a game is not the same thing as *being* a mummy and daddy. Children's awareness of realism and plausibility increases with age and is certainly in place by the alleged beginning of childhood, at the age of seven, although young children may still have some difficulty with particular plot devices and the stylistic techniques used to convey them, as Grant Noble's work shows. The writer to the *Radio Times* echoes Plato's belief that children cannot tell allegory from truth, in writing about children's supposed inability to cope with 'realism'. Modern televised drama, unlike some of the stories in Homer, is not allegorical, but 'realistic' – that is, it looks like real life. But 'realism' is a word for a theatrical or literary style; it is no more 'reality' than allegory is. It is a way of representing reality through dramatic scenes which may look and sound like a playground in a normal school, but which have, in fact, been carefully written, rehearsed and staged to create a theatrical impression of such a playground. Like playing mummies and daddies, it is 'pretend.' Just as Plato did not believe that children could tell allegory from literal truth, the letter writer believes that children cannot tell realism from reality.

This argument was strongly refuted by another writer to the *Radio Times* in the same correspondence, a 14-year-old girl who loved *Grange Hill*, found it 'very lifelike indeed' but was able to point out, 'I realise it's all a story, and a very enjoyable one'. This girl summed up why stories, though they are 'only' stories, have such value for children:

> I really identified with the children, especially in the first series when I was a second year and all my first year experiences were fresh in my mind. Then, in the second series, I was already acquainted with the pupils as though they were friends of mine. My sister (12½) and I hardly ever missed an episode and we

really worried about the pupils when they got into trouble. I must confess, I shed a few tears when Simon had to leave.

She was able to identify with the characters in the series, while being aware that her emotional reactions were not as appropriate as they would have been at a real parting: 'I must confess . . .'

The third assumption, that 'good' is what adults decide is good for children is perhaps best answered by this same 14-year-old, who points out the inadequate basis on which adults often make their judgements about what children enjoy. She stakes a firm claim for children being allowed to have their own tastes, free from adult interference:

What really infuriated me was the amount of adults who wrote in complaining about how bad it was. I'd like to know how many of them saw the whole series through, or just saw a number of (or even one) episodes. I'm not saying that adults are not allowed to watch our programmes, but it was written for us, the children, the pupils at schools like Grange Hill, who really understand what they're like.

This determined insistence on keeping the boundaries between childhood and adulthood clearly defined, with adults only being 'allowed' to watch *Grange Hill* on sufferance, ought to strike a chord of sympathy with Neil Postman, who wrote so pessimistically:

Everywhere one looks it may be seen that the behavior, language, attitudes and desires – even the physical appearance – of adults and children are becoming increasingly indistinguishable.

The irony is that Postman blames television for destroying the barriers between adults and children, whereas 14-year-old Michelle, quoted above, is using a favourite television programme to mark out the boundaries between childhood and adulthood. To her, programmes popular with children are 'ours'. What right, she seems to be saying, do people like Professor Postman have to make pronouncements on her territory?

This is a question worth asking. There seems some inconsistency in an argument which defends childhood by so persistently ignoring children. In the whole of Postman's book there is not one quotation from or reference to specific children that he has spoken to or studied. Of the many people who have served or studied children professionally, only Jean Piaget gets a brief reference. If the culture of childhood is to be defended from the inroads of adult commercialism and tawdriness and brutality, it will need to be done by adults who are prepared to work for and with children, and who acknowledge their existence. Commercialism, tawdriness and brutality, and worse things, such as institutionalised racism, existed before the television age in modern American society, as British children, studying for GCSE *The Great Gatsby* (1920s), *To Kill a Mockingbird* (1930s), and *Death of a Salesman* (1940s), will be aware. If the behaviour and values of adult America are not fit to lay before the young, shooting the messenger that brings the bad news will not fool children, nor will it adequately protect them.

Television as a drug

The second major school of thought about the evils of television takes an almost opposite view from Postman's. In her book, *The Plug-In Drug*, Marie Winn argues that the content of television is completely irrelevant. Watching adult sexual behaviour and adult violence is no different from watching *Sesame Street* or *Camberwick Green*, and thus, presumably, cannot be corrupting in the way that Postman fears. In her first chapter, headed 'It's not what you watch', she argues:

> Certain specific physiological mechanisms of the eyes, ears and brain respond to the stimuli emanating from the television screen regardless of the cognitive content of the programmes.

Despite a lengthy, quasi-scientific account of hemispheric specialisation in the brain, Marie Winn produces very little scientific evidence for this assertion. Her book abounds instead with anecdotes about children whose parents cannot drag them away from the television set, and are thus presumed to be hopeless addicts of the TV 'drug', but these have all been carefully selected to support her case, and do not constitute any kind of representative sample of television viewers. Their problems can also be interpreted differently.

There is the mother of the seven- and five-year-old boys, who complains, 'I don't need the TV as a babysitter at 3.30 when the kids come home from school . . . Unless I dream up something terrific for them to do, they don't just want to play. They pester and pester me to let them watch.' There is the hospital visitor who couldn't distract the six-year-old boy she was visiting from the television set: 'I went on desperately reading stories, playing cards . . . telling jokes because I was determined not to let that damned set win.' There is the mother whose 'pattern' was disrupted because her children wanted to watch *Jeannie* from 5.30 to 6.30 and 'our dinner-time was 6 o'clock . . . I'd tell the kids that if they insisted on watching *Jeannie* they'd have to turn it off when dinner was ready.'

Winn's catalogue of parents setting up battlegrounds for themselves on which they almost certainly could not win, reveals more about the confusion of parents over how to control their children than it does about television's supposed addictiveness. Television is like other famous battlegrounds of child-rearing: food and toilet-training. If parents take a confrontational position over it, they are almost bound to lose. Children know what they want and do not want to eat; they know when they're being got at over having to sit on the pot; they know what they enjoy and what they want to go on doing. Although mother knows best – that greens are good for you, that being clean and dry is nicer than being wet and dirty, and that watching television is bad – children know better, and they can hold out longer.

The wise parent does not take a confrontational position: she takes her sons out for a walk after school, then sits down and watches the television with them while they all have a cup of tea or a drink together. She then gets on with making the dinner while they do what they want to do, having made sure that there are plenty of alternative activities in the room with the TV set. (The wise parent therefore has a very untidy sitting room.) The wise parent serves dinner at 6.30, after *Jeannie* is finished. The sensitive hospital visitor accepts that a six-year-old boy with his leg in plaster may not be in an optimum condition for playing cards with well-meaning do-gooders, and sits with her arm round him, giving him an occasional cuddle, while he watches his programme. Winn does in fact acknowledge that the problem of excessive TV watching is primarily one of parental control when she describes the case of another mother who discovered that 'When I deliver an ultimatum with real conviction, it works!' When she told her children that morning television watching had to stop, they accepted it. 'That's the most exciting thing I learned as a mother.' It seems sad that there was nobody else in this mother's life who could have set her an example, or even just told her, of how to behave like an authoritative adult. This story is as much an indictment of the isolation in which so many women have to bring up children, as it is of television.

In her chapter, 'Hooked parents', Winn implies that television-watching is responsible for 'parents' steady loss of control as they gradually withdraw from an active role in their children's upbringing'. This would carry more conviction if Winn were to supply evidence that, in all other circumstances, the parents she quotes were authoritative and decisive. If she could show us that these parents were confident in their ability to get their children to sleep, be weaned, use the toilet, stop hitting other children, keep their rooms tidy and to get up in time for school, her argument against television would be powerful indeed. But as letters to agony aunts down the ages show (see Christina Hardyment's book, *Dream Babies*), parents have always dithered and frequently failed in these situations. As with Postman, Winn's attempt to make television a scapegoat for difficulties that are endemic to the hard labour of looking after children, can be dangerous. It can lead us to ignore all the other causes of these difficulties: simple inexperience, marital disharmony, economic hardship, unavoidable personality clashes between individuals and unhappy experiences in parents' own childhoods, to name only a few. How easy childrearing would be, Winn seems to be saying, if only there were no television. And how wrong she is.

The main burden of Winn's case that television is a drug is her argument that the processes involved in television watching are purely physiological: she compares viewing the changing pictures of television with 'staring into a flickering fireplace'. This, she argues, is an example of 'a non-verbal form of mental operation: the mind receives the changing movements of the flames – the visual stimuli are obviously received by the brain's sense receptors – and yet no verbal manipulations occur'. Winn makes a distinction between verbal and non-verbal information processing which is rather difficult to support. She argues that pictures and visual stimuli are devoid of the kinds of meanings carried by words (an argument also proposed by Postman). One only has to think of examples of powerful images in film, such as the final shot of Richard Attenborough's *Oh, What a Lovely War*, to realise what a fallacious argument this is. In this final shot, following a narrative which has shown the wiping out of every single male in one family during the First World War, the camera focuses on six white crosses. As the song *We'll never tell them* is heard on the soundtrack, the camera pans back to reveal more and more white crosses until the whole landscape of the screen, for as far as the eye can see, is filled with an ever-increasing mass of graves. There should be no need to translate the 'meaning' of this image, even for Marie Winn and Neil Postman. But if these people cannot grasp the statement being made by this shot, this does not prove that the image is not making a statement, only that some people cannot grasp it, and that children may need to be helped to interpret it.

There is a considerable body of theory, for example Gavriel Salomon's book, *Interaction of Media, Cognition and Learning*, on the symbolic functions of pictures – that is, the meanings that pictures carry over and above the simple referential aspects of the objects they show. There is also a substantial body of research in cognitive psychology on how pictorial and verbal meanings are integrated by viewers, readers and listeners – for example, the work of Kathy Pezdek in the United States. People 'read' pictures for meaning, as they do texts. Moving pictures, edited together in shots, scenes, sequences and whole narratives, need to be followed sequentially, as verbal sentences do, in order to be understood. Meaning and the cognitive processing of meaning are not only verbal, as both Winn and Postman argue they are; they are required by all symbolic systems, including film and television. The ways used by television to construct sequences of pictures follow narrative rules, which children need to learn to understand.

My own research showed that pictorial emphases, like close-ups, will be 'translated' into verbal emphases, like passive sentences, when people describe televised events. There seems to be regular interplay between pictorial and verbal forms and meanings, as people watch and listen to television. Winn's constantly reiterated statement, that TV watching is cognitively passive can be supported neither by the research literature, nor by the developmental fact that children, even when immobile, are never passive. Modern studies of infancy show that newborn babies are 'competent' and from birth will begin attempting to construct meaning and regularities in their lives. There is no evidence that these active attempts to make sense of stimuli – acknowledged by Winn in older children – are switched off when confronted with television. If children of a certain age seem to find something especially fascinating about television – a fascination which wears off as they get older, as discussed in Chapter 3 – we should pay them the compliment of trying to find out just what this fascination is.

If we feel that in watching television, children are neglecting other more interesting activities, more thought needs to be given about what these activities are supposed to be. In a world in which small children have to live in high-rise flats, and in which every available public space, including the streets, is dominated by traffic, it could be argued that it is not television that has restricted the lives of children, but the town planner and the motor car. We need to be honest with ourselves and admit, with Katharine Whitehorn (*The Observer*, 12 April 1987) that, without television, we would not necessarily be spending our 'entire time playing the recorder, making collages and reading one another's poems out loud'. Whitehorn is grateful to television programmes, like *Magpie*, *Blue Peter*, and later *Tomorrow's World*, *Horizon* and *Q.E.D*, for fostering her younger son's interest in electronics, now his career. She argues that grown-ups should insist that children should sit down and watch properly when good programmes are being shown: 'It ought to be shameful to admit that you missed *The Singing Detective* or *Yes, Prime Minister* or *Newsnight*.'

Whitehorn's argument is the antithesis of Winn's. She argues that content of television does matter and that what is required is television that 'moves the muscles of the mind'. Some British television, with its public service tradition, does attempt to do this, and British children's television certainly does – at the moment. But will it go on doing so when the forces of commercialism have allies like Marie Winn, who is prepared to write off the vast majority of child viewers?:

> The industry's cool indifference to the quality of children's television fare may indirectly prove to be more beneficial for children than the struggle of those who insist that fine children's programs be available at all times, since conscientious parents are more likely to limit their children's television intake if only unsavory programs are available.

Many conscientious parents would argue that this attitude is incredibly irresponsible; children deserve good television programmes, for the same reason that they deserve good books. Only by seeing what good television can be like, and how different it is from bad television, will children grow up into discriminating adults, able to guide their own children into making sensible choices for themselves.

5 | Television and the mind

Despite apocalyptic warnings about the dangers of television watching for mental processes, many parents see it as a source of information and education for their children. In a British study of young children carried out by James Halloran at Leicester University and described in *Pre-School Children and Television* (1974), 45 per cent of mothers questioned actively encouraged their children to watch television. Of these, the vast majority (80 per cent) did so because 'children learn things; it has an educational effect'. These mothers were not talking about overtly educational programmes; they were talking about programmes such as *Play School*, *Scooby Doo*, *Rupert Bear* and even *Doctor Who*. In another British study, carried out by Dr Cathy Murphy in 1983, mothers listed some of the things they thought their children learned from pre-school television: concepts, such as numbers, letters and shapes; songs and rhymes; vocabulary; imaginative play; general knowledge; concentration; craft activities; games.

What mothers believe their children are learning from television, and what they actually do learn, are not of course the same thing. There can be an even wider gulf between what programme-makers believe about their programmes and how children actually respond. For example, the authors of the 1974 report on pre-school children mentioned above, James Halloran and his colleagues at the University of Leicester, quote a statement by the then head of children's programmes at the BBC, Monica Sims: 'What would make me happiest would be if they went away; if we could stimulate them enough to go away and do something creative themselves.' However, the researchers noted: 'During the entire period of observation, we did not find one single child that was motivated by television to do things, draw pictures, make models etc.' A similar unwillingness was found by Cathy Murphy in her 1983 study of pre-school children; and Grant Noble, in a study on *Blue Peter* carried out in the 1970s and reported in *Children in Front of the Small Screen*, also found that children did not respond to the invitation to make a model, which they found quite difficult. But where children are specifically invited to respond, they will do so (see Chapter 10).

Nevertheless, as Halloran points out: 'This does not mean that children are totally unresponsive to such a stimulus.' Pre-school children do need the help of adults if they are to make or do something. Murphy found that over half the mothers she interviewed had 'done or made things based on programme ideas' and slightly fewer than half had 'used books or materials linked to programmes'. Television, like other media, does not necessarily work in directly observable ways to have an influence and it may take time for the constant exposure to creative ideas to have an effect.

One problem is that there is a dearth of research on children's reactions to television once they reach school age. It is also difficult to follow these reactions in the same children over a long period of time. The distinction between education and entertainment is not so marked at the pre-school stage. Once children are at school, school subjects are seen as education and television becomes entertainment. Educational performance is extensively monitored and reported on – and will be even more exhaustively researched when universal testing is introduced into British schools. But leisure-time activities, which contribute a great deal to what children know and to how they develop their skills, remain a neglected research area. There is no logical reason why older children should not continue to learn from their entertainment, just as younger children do. Yet, despite the existence of some studies into children's cartoons, such as the one carried out in Australia by Bob Hodge and David Tripp in *Children and Television*, discussed below, entertainment programmes arouse much less interest than educational ones, except, of course, for arousing adult disapproval.

It is possible that many professional educators and researchers still share the attitude of a teacher reported by Hodge and Tripp:

> When a boy stood up to give his news to the rest, he began, 'On Sunday there was this film on telly and it was all about . . .' but the teacher interrupted with, 'Now come on Johnny, news is things that really happened to us, not things we saw on the telly'.

If this teacher had seen the effect that the death of Damon Grant had had on the child fans of *Brookside* in this household, she could never have said that telly was not about things that 'really happened to us'. The loss of a favourite character in a story can seem like a bereavement and, as such, has to be treated with appropriate sensitivity by adults. Given the brusqueness of the teacher's response, it is to be hoped that Johnny was not going to talk about such a loss. It is interesting, too, to speculate on whether the teacher's reaction would have been different had it been a book Johnny had spoken of, rather than a film.

One possible reason for the acceptability of the accusation that television turns children into passive telly addicts could be this dismissive attitude to television-viewing on the part of adults. For instance, as Hodge and Tripp point out, many teachers rarely watch what children watch and have little idea of what their pupils are talking about. This can make it difficult for teachers to keep control over a discussion about television. This is a pity, for such discussions can reveal and encourage many lively and critical responses, but they would require the teacher to get down onto the children's level and watch the same programmes that they do. Some adults may be reluctant to do this. People who have taken the trouble to observe and study child viewers have identified skills and knowledge which seem to be particularly associated with television, rather than with other media.

Attention to television

An accusation frequently made against television is that it 'hooks' children's attention, so that they will stare at it uncritically, regardless of what the programme is about. This is the basis of Marie Winn's strictures, described earlier. In a *Kilroy* programme on BBC Television in April 1988, the leader of a British teaching union stated his concern that many pre-school children were watching for most of the 24 hours – 'until 1.20 in the morning'. Such children, he argued, were coming into school unable to talk or relate to others because of the hours they spent mesmerised by the box. Nevertheless, it is difficult to find any reliable evidence for such uncharacteristic behaviour in small children. Very young children are, by nature, active and exploratory and many parents will testify that it is extremely difficult to get them to sit still for long periods. Studies which have observed children watching television, suggest that their visual attention to the screen is not continuous, but can be influenced by all sorts of factors, including what is happening on the screen, and also what is happening around them, especially if they are watching with other children.

If children are left for long hours in front of the TV set, the question needs to be asked: Why do their parents let this happen? Are these parents having a generally difficult time exerting their authority as was the case with some of the people described by Marie Winn? A particularly pertinent question would be about the mental and social state of the mother. Is she socially isolated? Is she hard-up? Does she lack resources, facilities, ideas, friends, practical help, for encouraging her toddlers to do other things? Is she depressed? (A study of several hundred families with pre-school children carried out by psychologists from Great Ormond Street Hospital in the London Borough of Waltham Forest in the 1970s found that as many as two thirds of the mothers suffered from depression.) If, as is quite likely, the answer to most of these questions is 'Yes', then complaining about the amount of time that the children watch television is a pretty inadequate response to the family's problems.

In any case, the word 'attention' is often loosely defined. Traditionally, in writing and research about television, it is used to mean the direction of the visual gaze to the screen: attention is when you're looking at the TV, a drop in attention is when you're not looking at it. This is hardly an adequate account. In the first place, it is possible to look at something without really registering what is going on: looking doesn't necessarily mean seeing, and seeing doesn't necessarily imply meaningful scanning, noticing and understanding. All these processes need to take place before we can say that a child is really 'attending' to television. In the second place, it is possible to pay attention to the messages of television while not looking at all – that is, children can listen to the soundtrack while visually attending to other things like toys. We need to bear this in mind in evaluating horror stories about the number of hours young children watch television. Assuming these hours are accurately reported (and the official BARB viewing figures only begin with four-year-olds so we can't automatically asssume that), these hours only represent the time the set is on, not the time the children spend actually looking at it. A number of studies have shown that sound effects, loud music and 'peculiar or non-human voices', as American researchers Aletha Huston and John Wright wrote in an essay in 1983, can be just as important, if not more important, than visuals, in attracting children's attention to television. Sound has a great deal of what they call 'perceptual salience'.

Perceptually salient features are aspects of a TV programme (or, indeed, of any event) which make people sit up and take notice, because of their intensity, their movement, their novelty or their incongruity. On television, they include physical activity, rapid cutting, scene changes, special effects and the sound features mentioned above. Wright and Huston quote studies to argue that, at first, very young children's attention is influenced primarily by such noticeable 'formal' features, but that, as they get older, children learn to expect that features like changes of scene, or loud music should be associated with meaningful developments in plot or content. One study found that children were better able to understand programmes where 'salient' features coincided with important content, and this was particularly so the younger the children. In other words, children do come to expect that sudden bursts of music, or rapid action, or changes of scene and shot, ought to mean something; they should not be introduced for their own sake.

This is an important point not always appreciated by people making programmes. Because there is plenty of evidence that striking images, zappy editing styles, and unusual sound effects attract visual attention to the screen (and also, surely, because such things must be lots of fun to play with in the studio), it is assumed that these things must be added to any programme in order to make it 'exciting' or 'interesting'. This ignores the deeper meanings of the word 'attention', mentioned above, which are about trying to make sense of what is going on. An eminent British psychologist of the 1930s, Frederick Bartlett, coined a memorable phrase about how people cope with the bombardment of information all around them; he said we are constantly making 'effort after meaning'. Studies of newborn infants show that this effort after meaning begins at birth. If flashy visual techniques are not intelligibly associated with meaningful events or dialogue on television, they will simply be confusing, and ultimately lead to a drop in attention. They will thus have the opposite effect to the one intended: that is, of capturing the viewer's interest.

Some Japanese research on television, carried out in 1987 with very young children (two-year-olds) found that these toddlers made efforts after meaning in the way they gave their attention to television programmes. They were most attentive to aspects that made sense in their own human terms: to human characters, women's voices, and to animals. They were not impressed by camerawork such as panning, zooming and shifting. They preferred movement carried out, as in life, by people. These tastes were contrary to adult predictions about what the toddlers would enjoy watching. American research reported in 1980 to the International Communication Association has found that non-salient features of television, such as dialogue spoken by child actors, also increased attention in child viewers. Again, it seems reasonable that listening to other children speaking would be of great interest to children themselves; child dialogue makes sense in their terms.

These findings about children's attention have important implications about the way programmes for children should be made. They suggest that trying to 'hook' children with lots of technical tricks, which don't bear much relation to plot or character, could be counter-productive. We also need to remember that children's expectations of television will vary, depending on the sort of television they are used to. American children (on whom most of the research has been done) almost certainly grow up to expect lots of zappy editing and frequent interruptions for commercials, because that is what American television is like. British children may have very different expectations, and hence experiences, of 'attending' to television. We still await some British research on attention, comparable to the American research. But given that British children grow up with more slowly paced programmes than American ones, their attentional behaviour may be different from that of American children. I have certainly seen six- and seven-year-olds absolutely spellbound

71

by one 'talking head' during the BBC's *Jackanory* series. Tony Robinson's solo re-telling of *The Odyssey*, in *Odysseus, the Greatest Hero of them All*, in 1987, had more pulling power than any number of zappy cartoons. Faces and voices are the first things to hold a baby's attention. This taste does not change as children grow up – and television, with its powers of close-up, is uniquely capable of satisfying children's perennial fascination with the way human beings look and sound.

Televiewing skills

Many people have criticised television for not being as demanding, for example, as reading as a cognitive skill. Obviously, watching the dramatised serial of *Oliver Twist* on television does not require as much mental effort as reading Dickens's floridly written 19th century prose – an effort that, even in the 19th century, vast numbers of adults would not have bothered with nor have been able to make. But even for a keen reader who is under ten, *Oliver Twist* is too difficult to read. Television can offer a story which has considerable meaning for young children, in a form which they can understand. It can introduce the name of Dickens to millions of potential future readers who otherwise might not have heard of it at all. And the same argument applies even more powerfully to lesser-known writers. Furthermore, stories in televised, or filmed form can offer advantages which purely verbal versions do not have.

Laurene Krasny Brown, an American researcher who has compared children's responses to stories in different media, describes in *Taking Advantage of Media* a study with six- to ten-year-olds in which some children were shown a picture book version of a folk tale and some were shown an animated film version. Both versions were identical in plot, illustration style, text and narration. The children who saw the film were better at recalling the actions of the story – what actually happened – than were the children who saw the book. They were also able to mimic the actions more successfully. Children who saw the film were not able to recall the author's precise words as well as the children who heard the story. However, they were stimulated to provide intelligent alternative words from their visual memory; instead of saying 'Ananse poured some water over his head', which was the original text, they used words like 'shaked' or 'sprinkled'. In the film version, this is what the character's action looked like. So instead of the conventional 'poured', these children came up with the more vivid word, 'sprinkled'.

There is plenty of evidence from studies with both adults and children that pictures help viewers to remember both sequences of events, and, interestingly, information that is spoken at the same time as the picture, more accurately. Pictures, particularly moving ones, underline the meaning of words and can make ambiguous statements clear. People make considerable efforts to integrate words and pictures so that they have a clear and accurate memory for what really happened. Sharp visual details will also be remembered, even where viewers have not made any particular effort to remember them. As Laurene Brown points out, a film 'visualises more of the story's active verbs . . . actions seen on film and television are more memorable than those described on radio'.

Pictures seem to survive particularly vividly in memory, but far from this accuracy being at the expense of verbal information, these vivid memories seem actually to aid verbal memory as well. In a study I did on memory for television pictures and words as part of my Ph.D. research, some people who were tested on two occasions, two weeks apart, remembered some details on the second occasion that they had not remembered the first time. In all cases, viewers said that what helped them to remember the words was summoning up a memory for the pictures.

Imagination

It is often said that television spoils children's own imaginations. By supplying them with ready-made pictures, they don't have to work so hard to supply their own images of characters or events. This may be true while they are actually watching; but later memories of events, which is what imagination works with (after all, all images come from something we have seen at some point), may be stimulated by television's own special techniques into producing more original and unusual work. Laurene Brown describes a study done with nine- and ten-year-olds who saw, or heard, the Grimm fairy tale, *The Fisherman and his Wife*. In the story a magic fish grants all the wishes of the fisherman's greedy and dissatisfied wife. Her last wish was to be 'like God'. Children were asked to draw a picture of the wife as she made her last wish. The children who'd seen the film version were much more likely to represent the wife's anger and dissatisfaction than were the children who'd only heard the story, because the viewers had seen the character's emotions visualised in close-up shots. The 'listening only' children hadn't really grasped the point that the wife was dissatisfied; they drew a character smiling and looking pleased with herself. They were also more likely to draw a full-length figure, the standard way in which children draw people, whereas the viewing children were more likely to draw a close-up of the face to emphasise the character's emotions, as the film had done. These children had also seen depictions of the character in full-length shots, so they could have based their drawings on these. But the close-up gave them the idea of getting away from the stereotyped, full-length way of drawing people, in order to convey emotion more effectively. The visual technique of the film had helped these children to realise the moral point of the story: that this woman was never going to be satisfied, no matter how many of her wishes were granted. Their drawings were correspondingly both more truthful and more original in style than those of the listeners.

Understanding the motivations and emotions of the characters is an important part of the imaginative response to stories; remembering the plot or the vocabulary, which can be well-facilitated by radio or printed versions, is not enough to show true understanding. An American study with six-year-olds published in 1973 tested the moral awareness of children, using identical stories which were either shown as a drama on video, or were read aloud. Both the video and the 'audio' stories were further subdivided into two versions. In one version, a child character was depicted knocking a bottle from the top of the supermarket shelf, because he was being mischievous. In the other version, his action was explained because he was trying to help his mother. The child's action was the same, but his motivation was different in the different versions. Both viewers and listeners were given the 'naughty' and 'good' versions and children were asked whether the child should be punished for knocking the bottle down. Children under seven are not supposed to have much 'moral awareness' in terms of understanding people's motives. Nevertheless, the children who'd seen the video version were able to distinguish between the 'naughty' action and the 'good' action and to say that the boy who was trying to help his mother should not be punished. The children who'd only heard the two stories were more likely to say that the boy should be punished, regardless of his intentions. Television drama can thus be used to illustrate moral dilemmas and subtleties more clearly than can text by itself, particularly for young children.

Critical awareness

As children get older, much more will be required of them than simply being able to understand, remember and reconstruct stories and information. They will be expected to have

some critical awareness of how well the story, or programme, or text, has been presented and to have more
sophisticated criteria for making their judgements. They will
be expected to be aware of the contribution of form, style
and technique to the way a film, or piece of writing works –
or doesn't work – and to be able to articulate their
judgements clearly. This is the purpose of media studies
in schools, of which more will be said in Chapter 8.
However, if children are not doing media studies in schools,
how can we be sure that they are not being overloaded or
manipulated by television's persuasive techniques when they
are watching purely for entertainment? An in-depth study of
600 five- to 12- year-olds carried out by Bob Hodge and
David Tripp in Australia, mentioned above, revealed that
'the bête noir of lobby groups, the cartoon, which has been
stubbornly supported by generations of children, turns out
. . . to be a healthy form, ideally adapted to children's
growing powers'.

Hodge and Tripp talked to children about a cartoon,
Fangface, which children very clearly identified as being part
of a genre with a long tradition: Fangface is a werewolf born
into a human family and children were able to see immediately that he was similar to characters in other cartoons they
had seen, such as *Scooby Doo* and programmes like *The
Incredible Hulk*, in which supernatural transformations take
place and in which there is a blend of myth and realism.
They were well able to distinguish the mythical aspects of
the story from the everyday ones, using what Hodge and
Tripp call 'modality judgements' – that is, judgements
about the degree of realism and truthfulness of the story.
Such judgements have to be based on a critical awareness of
story conventions in cartoons, as demonstrated by the two
nine-year-old boys quoted here:

> You can tell, say, if a cartoon character went into a movie, a
> different thing, it wouldn't fit in exactly . . . [it would] be the
> wrong colour and he wouldn't . . . he wouldn't look real.

These nine-year-olds were able to point out in answer to what must have seemed a rather idiotic question from the interviewer ('Why don't you think the cartoon was really true?'): 'You wouldn't see The Heap running about in the streets and Fangface changing and changing back again.'

Fantastic stories like these are common in books of fairy tales and folk myths, now considered respectable reading for children – at least if they involve reading. Yet such stories were not traditionally read; they were heard, and they served a useful function in showing, in a form accessible to children, the age-old conflicts between good and bad, light and dark, nature and culture that are the stuff of all good myths. Hodge and Tripp's approach draws heavily on linguistics and anthropology, as well as psychology and literary criticism, for interpretation of children's responses. Such interpretation is obviously beyond the scope of most parents and others working with children; indeed children would be very startled if their parents attempted it. But the study does demonstrate that when children are actually asked about popular programmes like cartoons, they do reveal critical responses such as awareness of genre, recognition of 'modality' and the moral differences between heroes and villains. As one boy put it: 'You don't really think about it if you aren't asked. If you aren't asked, you don't think about it again.'

This emphasises again the importance of television being seen in the context of a child's everyday life. If parents are concerned about the enthusiasm with which their children view apparently 'mindless' cartoons, talking to the children and getting them to 'really think' about them may be more productive in getting the child's brain working than pouring scorn on the programme, or switching it off. Cathy Murphy's 1983 study, mentioned above, found that pre-school children talked more about the programmes they watched when somebody watched with them and discussed what they had seen and heard. This shared interest and experience extended the range of conversations about the programme

77

between mothers and children. As Murphy puts it: 'The themes of pre-school television programmes are much less likely to be extended and elaborated unless the programme has been watched with an adult.' This suggests an important aspect of television which deserves more attention: the extent to which children and adults should watch together. If the adults in the child's life clearly disapprove of television-watching, opportunities for enrichment may be lost. If, on the other hand, the television is being used as a babysitter, so that children are watching alone, children may be more stimulated to talk about the programme afterwards, if asked, precisely because they know the adult has not seen it. Cathy Murphy points out that 'children often do not make an effort to be explicit when they know that an adult has seen what they have seen and, therefore, already knows the answers to the questions being asked'. Thus, a key point to emerge from such studies is that, if adults are concerned about the 'mindlessness' of television viewing, some of the answer to the problem lies in their own hands.

Practical skills

Many programmes on television show people how to make or do things. Many educational tasks require this too: both children and adults need to follow instructions to learn how to make models; set up experiments; put things in order; sew, cook, garden, build, repair and so on. How effective is television at practical demonstrations of this kind? Two researchers at Nottingham University, Cathy Murphy (who carried out the pre-school study mentioned above) and her colleague David Wood, studied a number of four- to eight- year-old children to compare how well they per-formed a model-building task, with different kinds of instructions. Their aim was partly to get away from the emphasis on verbal testing which characterised much of TV research. They argued that this can put very young children at a disadvantage; it can also inhibit older, inarticulate children.

Murphy and Wood divided the children into three groups. One group had to construct a wooden pyramid with no instructions at all. Another group had a set of black and white photographs showing the various construction stages, to guide them. A third group were shown a three-minute black and white film demonstrating the construction process. There were ten children from each age (four, five, six, seven and eight) in each group. Murphy and Wood found that the children who'd had picture or film instruction did very much better on the model-building task than did the children who'd had no instruction. But the children who'd seen the filmed demonstration did even better than those who'd had the pictures to guide them. This is all the more remarkable, because the film children had to remember what they'd seen. The picture children had the pictures to guide them all the time they were building. Even so, the film children had fewer errors, completed the task more quickly and more closely imitated the original instructions than did the picture group.

The film was particularly helpful to the youngest children. Four-year-olds who had seen the film were much more effective at the task than four-year-olds who'd used the pictures. Many four-year-olds who got no instructions at all simply refused to perform the task. Murphy and Wood argue that:

> It is clear that pre-school children are able to learn and recall more from a filmed presentation than some studies of film and televised instruction lead us to believe . . . Our findings lend support to the view that verbal recall may be an inappropriate and misleading method of assessing comprehension of events in very young children.

Verbal recall may also handicap some older children, who are shy or who have language difficulties. Because television is an active medium, showing events and changes in events as they happen, its potential for giving practical instruction could be more exploited. The kinds of practical tasks used by Murphy and Wood (similar to the reconstruction tasks carried out by Robin Smith in his study of montage, described in Chapter 2) may also be a better way of finding out how well children understand television than time-honoured techniques of question and answer, or discussion.

Acquiring knowledge

The view of Thomas Gradgrind, in Charles Dickens's *Hard Times*, that education was only about 'Facts', has long been abandoned by educationists and teachers. Modern teaching methods stress skills and processes – the intellectual means whereby children acquire information as well as the information itself. Thus, work involving problem solving, research, use of library resources, use of data bases, and co-operation with others has, thankfully, replaced rote learning in most modern classrooms. The educational soundness of these approaches is eloquently argued in Rachel Pinder's book, *Why Don't Teachers Teach Like They Used To?* Nevertheless, all learning has to be based on some factual information and the acquisition of facts is actually quite popular with children who provide large enthusiastic audiences for TV quiz programmes and who show themselves to be accomplished participants in quizzes like the BBC's *Beat the Teacher*. They are also very keen to use TV as a source of factual information, as the thousands of letters asking such questions as, 'Why do we need sleep?' and 'What is the largest spider in the world?' sent to programmes like *Corners* and *The Really Wild Show* demonstrate. Existing factual knowledge may also be quite important in determining how much new knowledge can be taken in. In *Learning from Television News*, a piece of research done at the North East London Polytechnic about how much adults remembered of TV news, those who had performed best on an earlier general knowledge test were also best at remembering the new information given in the news bulletins. It seems that, in the case of knowledge, to them that hath, more shall be given. Thus children who already know a lot about the world they live in may have an advantage in some learning situations.

The study of how much factual knowledge children acquire from television has not been as popular as studies of the mental processes children use to learn from television, despite evidence that children often say they learn things from it and parents, such as those in Murphy's 1983 sample, cite 'general knowledge' and 'extending their horizons' as important functions of television for their children. I carried out a study on *Corners*, the BBC general knowledge programme for five- to seven-year-olds, based on questions sent in to the programme by children themselves. In this case, the producers themselves were keen to find out whether the information in their programme was being effectively got across to their target audience. I showed an episode of the programme to different groups of six-year-olds, seven-year-olds and a 'control' group of 11-year-olds who were assumed to be too old to really enjoy the programme, but who would probably be able to remember a lot of it because of their greater knowledge and experience.

The programme was 20 minutes long and consisted of nine items which answered children's questions about a variety of topics: the longest word in English; the longest name; how leaves grow; police patrols on a motorway; the Thames flood barrier; conditions on the moon. There were questions about how many babies are born each year and how many species of fish there are – plus some jokes, a demonstration of a trick, and a puzzle at the end of the programme. The information in the programme was thus quite tightly packed – and yielded 30 questions for my study which children were asked to answer (the younger children answering orally and on a one-to-one basis) after the programme was over.

As expected, the 11-year-olds remembered much more of the programme's information than the younger children, but they did not like it as much (emphasising the important point that liking and learning are not always equated and that low ratings don't necessarily mean that viewers aren't gaining benefits from a programme.) The six-year-olds remembered about 31 per cent of the programme's information, the seven-year-olds around 43 per cent and the 11-year-olds around 61 per cent. We were particularly interested in how well the children learned from two comparatively long and complex items in the programme – one about how leaves make food from light (photosynthesis) and the other about conditions on the moon, which explained the workings of gravity. The questions were closely related to the way the material had actually been presented in the programme, for instance: 'What will happen to the seeds Simon put under the box?' and 'Why could Simon and Tracey jump higher on the moon?' Thus, if any of the children already had prior knowledge of photosynthesis or gravity, the questions would be testing their ability to apply that knowledge to this new situation. And if they had no knowledge of the fact that plants grow towards light, or that gravity is less on the moon than on earth, correct answers to the questions would demonstrate that they had learned this from the programme.

For both these complex items, the younger children scored well above their average scores for the whole programme – and this difference was more than twice as great as it was for the older children: over 7 per cent for six- and seven-year-olds, 3 per cent for 11-year-olds. Although there were other parts of the programme that they found difficult to remember, particularly information involving large numbers, the younger children do seem to have acquired not only factual information from this edition of *Corners*, but also an enhanced understanding of scientific processes. *Corners* is intended to be an entertainment programme, but it is in the happy tradition of progressive education and children's television in this country which argues that learning can be fun. The children found it very enjoyable; their behaviour while watching was attentive, responsive and appropriate – for instance, laughing at the jokes, and answering the questions in the puzzle with which every programme ends.

Sesame Street had rather more didactic intentions. It was launched in the 1960s, after extensive co-operation between producers and researchers. Its aim was to teach children, in particular deprived children, numbers, letters, shapes, colours, signs and general knowledge, as well as less tangible values of tolerance and co-operation, and to use the sophisticated techniques of commercial television in doing so. Research done on the programme in America (*Sesame Street Revisited*) showed that children did indeed learn from *Sesame Street* and that, the more they watched, the more they learned, although watching the programme did not close the gap between working-class and middle-class children as the programme's originators had hoped. Research done in Israel by Gavriel Salomon in the early 70s, had the unique opportunity to study the effects of the programme on a population of children who'd never seen television at all. Television was introduced in Israel at that time. He found that the children's uptake of knowledge was related to what he called 'skill mastery', that is, the increasing ability to make sense of the programme by learning to understand its techniques. Thus the Israeli children, like the American children, learned more, the more they watched – and they also learned more if their mothers watched with them.

Both these studies demonstrate the interactive relationship between factual knowledge and skill – process and product – in learning. They also demonstrate again the part that familiarity with the medium and viewing companionship can play in increasing what a child gains from television. Salomon argues that different mental skills can be facilitated by the techniques of different media. He found, for instance, that children who were good at understanding the relationship of parts to wholes – being able to fit a missing detail into a picture, for instance – learned well from techniques that used cuts to close-up to convey information. In research

83

I carried out on learning from news, reported in *Journal of Educational Television*, I found that adolescents generally remembered less of the news than adults did. But when the same news was presented in a version with more frequent cutting, teenagers did as well as adults. Adults did much better when there was less cutting in the film. It may be that adolescent children, who have grown up with television techniques, don't try to map them onto pre-existing verbal structures as adults try to do. In my research, where cutting didn't correspond to verbal sentence structures, adults seem to have found this distracting and disruptive. Teenagers seem to be better than adults at 'parallel processing', as Patricia Marks Greenfield suggests in her book *Mind and Media*. Parallel processing enables the mind to take in different streams of information at the same time without one stream interfering with another. The adults in my experiments seemed to be trying to integrate the two streams – the verbal and the visual – and when they were out of step this integration wasn't so easy, so comprehension and recall suffered. This does not mean that programmes made for adolescents should be disconnected and indifferent to meaning: we all need to learn to integrate information.

Techniques such as cuts and close-ups seem to play a part in how people understand and organise the information they are receiving, and this can interact with different character-istics in viewers, such as their individual mental aptitudes and their age. Such evidence emphasises that any medium with its own sophisticated techniques for presenting inform-ation – as all media have – will invite an intelligent response in viewers, in which they attempt to make sense of the medium's codes and symbols and to use them appro-priately. TV viewers will, from an early age, monitor, acquire and utilise these techniques to help them make sense of the information they are receiving. There is no evidence from anybody who has taken the trouble to look, ask and properly analyse, that watching television is a 'mindless' activity – for children, or for anybody else.

6 | Television and violence

During the past few years, there has been a mounting chorus of public concern and debate about the effects of television violence, particularly on children. In an *Evening Standard* article in February 1988, TV playwright Ian Curteis castigated the 'flood of contagious violence on our screens' and demanded more legal control over broadcasters who 'scorned their social and moral responsibilities by projecting chainsaw massacres into our children's viewing time'. A look again at the figures given in Chapter 3 for the most popular programmes with children show that chainsaw massacres do not generally occur during children's favoured viewing times. This article was headed, apparently without irony, 'Let's knock some sense into the programme makers', which raises straight away the double standards of much of the press comment on televised violence.

A couple of weeks later, in the same newspaper, columnist Peter McKay proudly recounted the pre-television exploits of himself and his boyhood friends:

> When I was a boy we made carbide guns . . . My eldest brother, aged 14, used to lock .22 bullets in a vice and explode them . . . once from 15 paces he shot me through a fleshy part of the hand . . . We . . . shot air rifles at each other – one boy, Mansel Ritchie, lost an eye I remember – and created a huge explosion with a big balloon full of helium that caused a neighbour's two horses to bolt.

The popular press's glorification of violence is not confined to feature articles either. In an article in *The Listener* in 1985

I pointed out that an issue of the *Daily Mirror* which criticised the 'bloodbath' of violence on TV, devoted 56 per cent of its own news coverage to stories about crime, violence, pain or sexual deviation.

Violence sells newspapers; it also attracts large audiences of TV viewers – 25 per cent more than the average peak-time audience, according to IBA research published in January 1988. Most parents in this study (60 per cent) thought that watching violent television made children more aggressive. On the other hand, 75 per cent thought that *The A Team*, *Magnum* and *Minder* were harmless even for under-fives. Hardly anybody thought that such programmes were harmful for 11- to 15-year-olds. While there does seem to be a generalised concern about the effects of violence on children, these effects seem to depend on a number of factors: what sort of violence we are talking about; what the outcome of the violence is; what sort of children we are talking about (including whether they are our own, or other people's), and what sort of home background they come from. We also need to remember the other sources of information about violence in children's lives, including popular newspapers. If children behave aggressively, how can we be sure that television is to blame?

Research on violence

In the 1960s, an American researcher, Albert Bandura, seemed to demonstrate that children who'd seen violent behaviour on film were more likely to be aggressive in their play afterwards; the measure of aggression was their willingness to attack an inflatable 'Bobo' doll, as seen on screen. Underlying this research was the theory that children model-led their behaviour on what they saw others doing, regardless of other constraints such as knowing that such behaviour is 'naughty' – the 'copycat' view of television effects. Other researchers, such as Kevin Durkin, working more recently in

Britain, have argued against this 'hypodermic' model – the idea that what goes in automatically comes out again in the same form. An IBA study in 1987 suggested that children's own personalities and aspirations (the sorts of characters they wanted to be like) affected their viewing tastes – with more aggressive children, particularly in the ten- to 12-year-old age group, having a greater preference for action adventure programmes. These researchers suggested that personality affected choice of viewing, rather than the other way around. Other researchers have pointed out that, just because children behave more aggressively in the short term after seeing a violent action in an experimental situation, this does not mean they would do the same thing at home. It also does not demonstrate that there will be a long-term effect on the sorts of people they become.

A long-term study carried out in America, reported in 1977, looked at the relationship between aggressive behaviour in nine-year-olds and the viewing of violent television programmes, and then studied the same children ten years later, at the age of 19. Boys who had liked violent television at nine were more likely to be rated as aggressive by other people in their age group than children who had not had such a taste for violent television in childhood. This does look like a long-term effect – but still does not settle the question of the 'direction of effect': does television make children violent, or do children who were already violent prefer to watch violence on television? It also does not explain why boys should be more affected than girls. A later study carried out by Jerome and Dorothy Singer of Yale University, with nursery school children, seemed to show that, over a year, violent television viewing did increase the amount of aggression (as measured by, for example, 'physical attacks . . . pushing, knocking over of each other's blocks'). This could not be related to the child's initial personality, as children who were aggressive at the beginning of the year did not watch significantly more action adventure programmes at the end of the year, whereas children who watched lots of action adventure at the beginning of the year, had become more aggressive by the end of the year. This study also found similar evidence of aggression among both boys and girls – the authors pointed out that there had been a 'marked increase in the availability of superheroines' such as Wonder Woman, Bionic Woman and Charlie's Angels. Nevertheless none was very aggressive.

It will be obvious from the above brief accounts, that most of the research on children and televised violence comes from America where there is both a much higher level of violence in society as a whole, and where there is far more violence on TV. It will also be obvious that much of the evidence is conflicting, with some findings suggesting that a violent personality comes first and this leads to a taste for violent programmes, and other findings suggesting the reverse. Although it is very difficult to 'prove' that television causes violence, I do not share the view of some ultra-libertarians that therefore it doesn't matter how much violence is shown. If already-violent personalities, like watching violent programmes, it does not follow that this taste should be indulged. If these people are violent already, this is a problem for society, television or no television. Why legitimise their violent tendencies by showing them material that appeals to their aggression and cruelty?

That said, there are times when violence must be shown for the sake of realism and truth, and awakening people's consciences. I myself may not like this, because I am an extremely squeamish viewer. However, although I now find it very difficult to watch scenes of violence and suffering, this sensitivity has developed since I was an adult. As a child I was more robust – and this is an important point to bear in mind in considering the 'effects' of televised violence on the young. A childish fascination with gore and melodrama does not mean that a person will be a sadist when he or she grows up.

Another problem with applying American findings to this country is that in the US there is also a shortage of good programmes made especially for children, as reported in a paper given by Peggy Charren of ACT to the British Film Institute's conference on Television and the Family in 1987. The result of this is that children who want to watch television are virtually forced to watch a great deal of material not specifically suited to them. Thus, we need to be cautious about applying the findings of American research to this country, with its much stronger tradition of public service broadcasting, and its commitment to children as a special audience, with their own needs, dating back to Lord Reith. The pressures of commercialism, which lead to more violent programming because of the popularity of action adventure series and their power to pull in audiences, are also less great in the UK than in America.

This could change when broadcasting in this country is deregulated – that is, removed from the almost exclusive control of the two main broadcasting authorities, the BBC and IBA – and becomes open, through satellite and cable television, to all sorts of influences from outside Britain. This is a matter of legitimate anxiety to those concerned with children and their needs. Material likely to be seen by children needs to be regulated, by people with children's interests at heart, not deregulated. As Clare Mulholland, whom I spoke to at the IBA, points out: 'The idea of a Broadcasting Standards Council and the idea of a free market in broadcasting are absolutely irreconcilable.' Nevertheless, both these ideas are being pursued by the present government. In the meantime, the research from America may serve as a warning of what might happen here, if their broadcasting model is adopted, though the kind of society children live in, as well as the kind of broadcasting it produces, must influence the impact of television content: Mallory Wober, Deputy Head of Research at the IBA, has pointed out that 'Japanese television has a great deal of crime and violence in it. Yet research shows that children in Japan are less aggressive than children in other countries.' It would seem that other factors than television influence whether children in different societies behave aggressively or not.

The debate about violence can be conducted at a policy level, with both the BBC and IBA producing tighter guidelines about violence on television and the government and moralistic critics calling for greater controls and a Broadcasting Standards Council. The fact remains that what is finally agreed to be a legitimate level of violence will continue to be shown on television, both in the news and in drama; there will also continue to be more of it late at night, after the 9pm watershed, when parents are assumed to be responsible for sending their children out of the room or to bed. Thus the problem of violence and its possible effects on children will not go away, no matter how stringent the guidelines drawn up may be.

Coping with violence

There is a good deal of pain, suffering, cruelty and warfare in the world, just as there always was before television came along, and it is right that television should report it, both as news and in dramatised form. The dilemma of how to represent truthfully the essence of a GCSE text in a schools TV programme, was expressed by producer Bruce Jameson at a conference on books on television organised by the Children's Book Circle in February 1988. The book was *Talking in Whispers* by James Watson and it dealt with the experiences of a teenage boy during the military coup in Chile which overthrew the Allende government. A central passage was about the boy being tortured with electric shocks; how could this be dramatised for pre-watershed daytime television, without sacrificing the horror of the situation? The producers eventually chose to focus the camera on the faces of the torturers while the buzzing of the electric current and the boy's screams were heard. This was a legitimate use of horrific violence, suggested rather than explicitly portrayed, in order to help children be more aware of the book's message. The producers of this schools programme argued that violent scenes such as this are essential to the educative process of understanding the text and ought not to be repressed.

Not all violence represents a realistic portrayal of political injustice, as in this case. Conflict is the essence of drama and every genre – the Western, the police thriller, the war story, even family drama – will use the 'shoot-out', or the 'punch-up', as a symbolic way of representing good versus evil. The interviews carried out by Bob Hodge and David Tripp in their book *Children and Television* demonstrate that children as young as six understand the symbolic function of this kind of violence, particularly in cartoons, and can differentiate it from the real thing, as can be seen in the following exchange:

Interviewer What about if somebody gets killed on television?
George (aged six) Um . . . they're not really killed.
Interviewer They're not really killed on television?
George They're just pretend bullets and they just pretend they're killed and they get all dead on purposely.
Interviewer I see . . . And what happens in life when somebody gets killed?
George Um . . . they die.

All the children interviewed by Hodge and Tripp made similar responses, based on their awareness of the conventions of television drama. As the authors put it: 'The basis in every case was some recognition of the processes of media production – acting, pretending, use of tomato sauce, or some reference to the illusionism of actors and directors.' Where violence is being used in this symbolic way – and this is particularly so in the case of cartoons – children are able to remain undisturbed and unaffected by it because of its remoteness from reality. But, the researchers point out, this does not mean that they are unaffected by real violence.

The fear of violence

An American researcher, George Gerbner, has proposed that the primary effect of televised violence on viewers is not a tendency to become more violent themselves, but to become more fearful. Studies carried out by him and his team suggest that heavy TV viewers are much more likely to have what the researchers call 'a mean world' view of life than less heavy TV viewers. This raises again the problem of 'direction of effect'. It could be that more fearful people choose to watch a lot of television, rather than going out. These studies did not differentiate between different types of programme. A British study, reported to the International Television Studies Conference in 1986, found that people had different perceptions of violence depending on what type of programme it occurred in. The more remote the violence from their own lives (for example, in American crime series) the less disturbing they found it. However, other research which gives a different impression to Gerbner's was contained in a 1987 IBA Research Paper on children's television viewing and its relationship with 'confidence in the face of crime', which found, interestingly, that children who watched a lot of adult films and drama, including action adventure series, were more likely to express courage at the prospect of hostile acts being performed against them. They were also more likely to show bravery at the prospect of possibly unpleasant experiences like injections, or fun fair rides.

This all raises the complexity of children's reactions to violent material. An excessive concern for purely imitative effects can mean that we are less likely to look for the plus side – the possibility that 'aggression' is not always bad, and can be associated with physical bravery and the ability to face up to life's unpleasantness. An Australian study carried out in 1981 by Grant Noble underlines further the complexity of children's reactions. This study found that children with more mature and unselfish attitudes particularly enjoyed programmes featuring very selfish and unpleasant characters, such as J.R. Ewing in *Dallas*. The author suggests that 'J.R. is closely observed and acts as a model for "how not to behave" '. If children are only shown upright and unselfish characters performing beautiful and beneficial acts, their need for 'negative identification' – their need to recognise the kinds of people who should be disapproved of – will not be met. This kind of complexity of reaction, with children showing sophisticated moral judgements, will not be recognised so long as the debate about the effects of violence and 'bad examples' confines itself to a concern with imitation only.

Distressing and violent events on television can also help children to come to terms with their own fears and emotions – just as fairy stories and folk tales have always done. Grant Noble, who has done a great deal of research with children and television, goes so far as to describe television as the modern equivalent of folklore. When Damon Grant, the popular and attractive young son of one of the families in *Brookside*, was stabbed to death in an act of casual street violence, the effect on my eight-year-old daughter was devastating. Damon's death became the subject of conversation and concern within the whole family for several weeks. We all agreed (older siblings too) that Elinor should be allowed to continue to watch *Brookside*, with its harrowing, and brilliantly acted, scenes of family mourning and recrimination – and that we would support her through them. (Everyone else was upset as well.) She found her own ways of dealing with her emotion. Here is a letter that she wrote to me while I was in the next room:

Dear Mum, I think that Damon dieing in Brookside was awfal. I was crying because of it. The script writers should of thought before they had writen the script. I know Damon wanted to get out of Brookside, but they dident have to kill him out of it. Damon and Debbie could of gone to America to get out of it and have stayed there anyway lets change the subgect because I am crying. Here did you see Bread on Sunday, I did it was really good it was funny too . . . Today I am ill and I am at home I have got a cold and a cough. I saw Brookside last night and it was sad Ooopps I am getting back on that subdject, Yours sincerely, Eli Davies.

At eight, Elinor was well aware that *Brookside* was a soap opera, with special problems of writing out long-running characters when the actors wanted to leave. She knew there were alternative possibilities for writing out characters, such as sending Damon and his girlfriend Debbie to America. In this, she shows a high degree of what Hodge and Tripp would call 'modality judgement' – the ability to use her knowledge of media conventions in evaluating the programme. This does not diminish her grief at Damon's death and her identification with his family, but it enables her to put it into perspective. It was interesting, too, that she used another television programme, the comedy *Bread*, also about a Liverpool family, to cheer herself up: this represents another fictional alternative, the joky, lighthearted side of Scouse family life. When she realises that her emotions are carrying her away again, she is able to control them and to bring her lament to an end. Elinor, with three much older siblings, is an experienced soap opera viewer and these experiences seem to have taught her how to recognise and cope with the emotions aroused by fictional drama in a way that would not have been possible if she had had less familiarity with the genre. Her reactions are very similar to those reported in the Hodge and Tripp study and suggest the importance of children being taught how to evaluate television in its own terms. If television is dismissed by educationists and others as mindless and violent moving wallpaper, the kinds of valuable lessons learned by regular viewers like Elinor and six-year-old George (quoted above) will not be recognised. But they should be.

Video nasties

In the early 1980s a great deal of concern was generated, again fuelled by the tabloid press, about the apparent 'fact' that a high proportion of children as young as four had seen 'video nasties' – defined in the book *Video Violence and Children* by Geoffrey Barlow and Alison Hill as 'feature films that contained scenes of such violence and sadism involving either human beings or animals that they would not be granted a certificate by the British Board of Film Censors for general release for public exhibition in Britain'. A research project to find out the extent of child viewing of video nasties was set up by the self-styled 'Parliamentary Group Video Enquiry' (not, in fact, authorised by Parliament) and this purported to show that as many as 45 per cent of children of seven and over had seen a video nasty. The validity of this research was challenged by other researchers. For instance, Dr Guy Cumberbatch of Aston University gave similar question-naires to those used by the group to similar groups of children and found that 68 per cent of children claimed to have seen films that did not exist. Nevertheless, the research was sufficiently influential to help the Video Recordings Act to become law in 1984. This restricts the availability of videos for home use.

The research of the group, described in this book, includes psychiatrists' case histories, teachers' comments and survey material, for example, a survey carried out by the NSPCC on families they visited. The aim of the research was unequivocally to support the view, already held by members of the group, that violent films on video are bad for children and should be restricted legally. This makes the research suspect straight away, since it is difficult to imagine the group publishing findings that did not support its initial viewpoint. A further problem with the validity of the research is that material drawn from case studies of families who already, by definition, have problems because they have been referred to the NSPCC or a psychiatrist, cannot tell us anything reliable about the population as a whole. Obviously we are right to be concerned about the effects of violent videos on children; but if a child is already suffering abuse, nightmare reactions at sadistic videos are not to be wondered at and cannot be reliably attributed to the films alone.

Nobody concerned with children could relish the prospect of them seeing films such as *The Evil Dead*, in which, to quote the synopsis given in *Video Violence and Children*, 'Two demons repeatedly assault Ash and one has his eyes gouged out . . .', although it's possible to imagine that boys like Peter McKay's friends, who spent their time shooting and bombing each other, might find it rather tame stuff. The greater availability of video recorders, now owned by 61 per cent of families with children, has created a problem in increasing the likelihood of children seeing material that was never intended for them, either broadcast after the 9pm watershed, or available in video form. The key question is: what is the best way of protecting children from the harmful effects of such material? One thing is certain: elaborately orchestrated press campaigns, in which lurid-sounding films are given massive publicity, is not the ideal way. Many people who never knew of the existence of *Zombie Flesh Eaters*, and what happens in it, must have found out, thanks to the efforts of the Video Enquiry group.

There are a number of possible answers to this question. First, research needs to target vulnerable children and to try to explain why some children may suffer from such films and why others seem to be able to shrug their effects off. What factors, such as age, sex, personality, social background, other leisure activities, might influence how a child responds to ugly material? Obviously it is wrong to expose children deliberately to such films; reliable research methods need to be found to assess their impact without breaching ethical standards. There is a powerful case for good, open-minded research, in which the researchers do not start out with a preconceived idea of what they are looking for. The danger of this approach should be obvious: if you are absolutely convinced that video violence is the cause of, for example, sadistic fantasies in children's creative writing, you may overlook the possibility that these children may have other problems. Child sexual abuse is now recognised as being much more common than was once thought. Child-battering was only 'discovered' in the 1960s, although it must have gone on long before. If children are suffering, people who care about them must be alert to all possibilities. In scape-goating violent videos, unpleasant though they are, it may be fatally easy to ignore other culprits.

In the second place, the greater availability of the video places greater responsibilities on parents. Ultimately, the responsibility for what children watch rests with them. If parents do not care what their children see, or what effect it may have on them, those children are already at a disadvantage, television or no television. However, the evidence is that most parents do care what their children see. Just because some parents believe that *The A Team* is more appropriate viewing for their five-year-olds than worthier programmes like *Wildlife on One* does not mean that these parents are undiscriminating. Sitting together viewing *The A Team* at Saturday teatime may be valued for all sorts of reasons which can vary from family to family. Parents are responsible for their children – but it follows from this that they know their own children best. Legislation and guide-lines which do not take account of the views of all parents, as comprehensively and objectively elicited as possible, is not going to be much use to children or to families.

Finally, the role of the child in learning to defend him or herself from distress, should not be forgotten. We cannot keep children from seeing or hearing disturbing events. Thus, we need to understand more about the protective mechanisms that help children cope with these events: their 'modality' knowledge; their experience of life generally; above all the context in which their television viewing occurs

– their relationships with their families and with other people.

In their study of the relationship between aggression and television viewing in nursery school children, included in *Violence and the American Family*, Jerome and Dorothy Singer found a number of interesting interactions between family styles, aggression, TV viewing and characteristics in the children. Children who watched a lot of television and were also very aggressive (High TV/High Aggression) came from somewhat disorganised families where there was very little parental control; where there were very few other things to do, such as reading, music or outings; where the parents followed traditional sex roles, with the father taking little part in home-making activities, compared to other groups. These children also tended to have lower IQs (not, in itself, a cause of aggression, since children in other groups with high IQs were also very aggressive.) The families were more likely to be lower down the social scale – again, not a 'cause' of aggression, since lower-class families also occurred in Low Aggression groups.

The children in the High Aggression/Low TV watching group had the highest IQs of all (an average of 125). Their parents tended to be intellectual and professional and their lifestyles were characterised by high levels of activity, competition and individualism (autonomy). Perhaps not surprisingly, these households were described as 'disorderly in their daily routines'. The children took part in a great many 'self-directed varied activities by parents that preclude . . . much watching of television by children'. However, when the children did watch television, they showed a higher preference for action adventure shows than did children in the low aggression groups, which their parents didn't seem to mind about. This appeared to fit in with the generally competitive and frenetic pace of their family life. Like the children in the High TV/High Aggression group, these children were more likely to be smacked as a punishment by their parents (unlike the low aggression children) and were less likely to be rewarded with praise for good behaviour.

The children in the High TV/Low Aggression group (who watched a lot of television, but weren't aggressive) came from the most orderly and organised homes. These families had a wider range of other cultural activities and they used television in a positive way, encouraging children to watch more imaginative and educational programmes – which in America then consisted primarily of *Mr Rogers' Neighbourhood* and *Sesame Street*, but in this country would encompass a much wider range of drama, storytelling and music and magazine programmes. These children scored highest on tests of imaginativeness and thus were, as the researchers put it, 'in a position to limit the more direct influence of what they watch and instead translate it into fantasy and make-believe games'. The researchers point out that some psychological tests show imaginativeness is 'negatively related' to aggression, that is, that imaginative people are less likely to be violent people. The families in this group appeared to have harnessed television positively, but not restrictively, since their children were High TV watchers, and to have incorporated it into their highly harmonious lifestyles. (Findings for a Low TV/Low Aggression group were not reported.)

These findings give just a hint of the fascinating complexities of the origins of behaviour and how they are rooted in family style and personality, as well as cultural activities like television watching. No conclusive judgements about the effects of television on children can be made without this kind of detailed analysis of its relationship with other, much more influential factors in children's lives, such as their parents' cultural tastes and attitudes to punishment. Reading the Singers' accounts, there is little doubt about which of these households would be most pleasant to visit: the High TV/Low Aggression group. Yet the Singers end their fascinating account of their research with a, to me, quite unjustified harking back to the Golden Age literary model of harmonious family life, based on one parent, one child and a book. They acknowledge that 'television in the home is a delightful source of entertainment', but go on to say:

> We prefer for the growing child the image of a quiet moment at bedtime when an adult sits by the child's side and tells a story or reads from a book in a way that forces the child to stretch its own imagination amid warm surroundings. Herein we feel lies the best basis for developing a sense of trust and at the same time a broader ability for private creativity.

This is a pleasant image of the short period when a young child has a bedtime story to him or herself. But once this period has passed, are there to be no other models for warm family contact between adults and children, while imaginations are stretched? Reading is a valuable activity, but a private one. I would like to place against the Singers' image, an image of my own: I and my four children are watching *Brookside*. The topic of Damon's funeral comes up. My two daughters, aged eight and 15, are permanently at war with each other – but as eight-year-old Elinor's eyes fill with tears and the two boys look anxiously at me, 15-year-old Hannah opens her arms and Eli runs from my side to her sister's. The two of them sit with their arms around each other on the sofa, openly weeping, while Hannah explains the complexities of the dialogue to Elinor. The rest of us need say nothing, but we are sharing the experience just the same – something that would have been unlikely with a book. Eli will still have her chapter of *The Peppermint Pig* after *Brookside*. But it will not be a more valuable experience than the one she has just shared with Hannah and the rest of us – just a different one.

7 | Television and social attitudes

In her first book, published in 1967, *Cleaning Up TV*, Mary Whitehouse wrote of 'the tremendous impression' made on her by a 'clean-living' girl who, after seeing pre-marital sex discussed on television, announced that she now knew that: 'I must not have sex until I am engaged.' Mrs Whitehouse wrote: 'In a few brief words (these girls) had been won over to a sub-Christian concept of living. Was there any ground for imagining that the effect on young people all over the country who had heard this programme was any less far-reaching?' Mrs Whitehouse does not pause to answer her own question. If she *had* paused for an answer, it would have to be: 'Yes; plenty of grounds. What were these girls' attitudes to pre-marital sex before the programme? Did this one girl speak for them all? Were the girls she knew typical of all girls, all over Britain? How did she know? Did she canvass the views of any boys?' One could go on . . .

Mrs Whitehouse is only one, probably the most well-known one, of the many people who believe that television – even just one showing of one programme – has profound effects on children's attitudes to life, morality and other people, overruling all other influences for good. Ironically, this attribution to television of irresistible power over viewers' attitudes, is shared by commentators who, in other respects would not be seen dead in the same ideological corner as Mrs Whitehouse. In a 1984 essay entitled *Black Blue Peter*, media studies lecturer Bob Ferguson castigates the long-running children's magazine programme for being 'youthful, pure and good'. Ferguson claims that the 'discourse' of *Blue Peter* is 'essentially middle-class', it denies history and 'the struggle for change' and 'epitomises the naturalisation process by which ideology is conveyed and cumulative myths find their material forms'.

Ferguson is as indignant in his anti-imperialist stand against *Blue Peter* as Mary Whitehouse is in her disapproval of the 'sub-Christian' ethos of the BBC's *Meeting Point*. For both, television is at fault because it does not purvey what they believe to be appropriate ideological messages to the young. Neither quote evidence that the young are in fact being brainwashed in the manner they claim (apart from Mrs Whitehouse's anecdote). We are asked to believe, without even as many as half-a-dozen children being consulted, that Christian girls everywhere have been 'won over' to non-Christian morality; that *Blue Peter* viewers are being unquestioningly 'naturalised' into an imperialist ideology. Not 'may'; not 'could be'; 'are'.

Just as children should be educated not to accept unquestioningly everything they are told, so, in this chapter, some of the unsupported assertions about television's social and moral effects will be looked at critically, in the light of some of the evidence (and admittedly, there is not nearly enough of it) that has been gathered on the subject. This is one of the most difficult areas of all to study because people's attitudes are built up over a lifetime and children encounter 'moral' questions at every turn, not just on television. Judgements about right and wrong, good and bad, are made constantly, at home, at play with other children, at school, out shopping, through comics, books – and of course, through entertainment media like television, films and theatre. From the baby being told that she's 'Mummy's best girl' for agreeing to eat solid food, to the child being told that she mustn't talk to 'strangers', to the adolescent being criticised for the hairstyles of her friends, children are continuously exposed to procedures which show them what kinds of people and behaviour will meet with approval from the people around them, and what will not. As every parent and teacher knows, children's exposure to various social and moral norms does not mean that children will automatically agree to conform with them.

The situation is further complicated, because many forms of behaviour to which judgemental labels are attached, are not imposed by upbringing, but seem to 'come naturally'. This is obviously true of very early anti-social habits, like dirtying one's nappy or waking up in the night. But it also seems to be true of more sophisticated forms of behaviour. For example, all healthy children, everywhere, like to play. This may be inconvenient, untidy and noisy for adults, but even the grimmest of grown-up killjoys have not found a way of stopping children doing it. Similarly, much as we all deplore violence, there is plentiful evidence that many well-brought-up children go through a stage of liking to fight – boys particularly, though not exclusively. To disentangle the contribution of television (itself a kaleidoscope of different programme types) to children's social and moral attitudes is a task of daunting proportions.

Many studies have been made, and much has been written about television's 'effects' on attitudes. Of particular concern are violence (discussed in the last chapter); attitudes to race and gender; and sexuality. Some of these concerns come from opposite ends of the political spectrum: on the right are concerns about sexual morality, lax attitudes to discipline and authority, and violence. On the left are concerns about racism, sexism, and imperialist attitudes towards the rest of the world. In common is a concern that faulty ideology is embedded in much of television's output and that children are unquestioningly soaking it up, to the detriment of society. Implicit in such arguments is a belief that if children could only be exposed to programmes which exalted pre-marital chastity, or which showed the brutality and corruption of the British in India, they would immediately adopt the 'correct' ideological views and become virtuous revolutionaries forthwith.

It seems unlikely, from the historical evidence, that there will ever be a time when children will prefer *Eric, or Little by Little* to the *Boy's Own Paper*, or Walter the Softy to Dennis the Menace. Children do not like being preached at and the best children's writers are subtle in planting their messages, subordinating ideology (which dates extremely quickly) to the more lasting demands of a strong plot and characters. A good example is E. Nesbit's entertaining chapter on the visit of the ancient Babylonian Queen to Edwardian London in *The Amulet*. Arch references to Mrs Besant, an influential social reformer of the time, are completely meaningless to modern children. More relevant are the Queen's surprised comments on the degraded appearance of the London working-class:

> 'You'll have a revolt of your slaves if you're not careful', said the Queen. 'Oh no,' said Cyril. 'You see they have votes – that makes them safe not to revolt. It makes all the difference. Father told me so.'

Yet, even with a writer so attuned to children's tastes as Nesbit, it's doubtful that the political irony of this passage can be picked up by the average seven- to ten-year-old. When our children were young enough to enjoy *The Amulet* being read to them, they liked the Queen imperiously wishing that all the poor people could have enough to eat, but we had to stop and explain the passage about voting – which rather held up the flow of the narrative. By the time the children were 12 or so and had outgrown the story, the political point was clear – even clearer to the children, perhaps, than it was to Nesbit. As one teenager overhearing the story pointed out, she actually seems to be in favour of benevolent autocracy, rather than any genuine improvement in democracy for the workers. By 12, too, they were also able to be critical of the cosy middle-classness of *Blue Peter*, while still enjoying many of its items. When children's reactions to the social and moral messages of television programmes are examined, they often turn out to be different from those of adults – and to those expected by adults.

Attitudes to race

In a study published in 1984 David Buckingham, a media studies lecturer at London University, studied the reactions of secondary school pupils to a Thames TV programme on racism in the media, *The Whites of their Eyes*. The programme critically analysed different ways in which the media might seem to be racist, showing, in Buckingham's words:

> That racist jokes and comedy programmes show black people as primitive and inferior; that media images of the British Empire reinforce notions of 'natural' white superiority; that the representation of Third World Countries shows them as helpless and disorganised; and that black people in Britain are often depicted as criminals and troublemakers.

The aim of the programme was to open children's eyes to the ways in which media might encourage prejudice – but, as Buckingham found, the children responded in unexpected ways. In the first place, many did not appear to understand that the programme was talking about media attitudes to black people, not attitudes generally. Many of the white children felt that they were being personally criticised and 'got at'; they also resented the fact that no white people were shown in the programme. Interestingly, some black children criticised it on these grounds too. This resentment, for some white children, expressed itself in quite violently racist remarks in their questionnaire answers. Other basically well-meaning white children suggested that 'if blacks want to say things against the whites then it's up to them, but they've got to learn that we're going to say it back'. The programme's attack on situation comedies offended both white and black children, for whom such programmes were very popular. One group of black girls resented the programme on the grounds that it showed 'too many Africans'. As children of West Indian families, brought up in Britain, they felt that the programme would encourage white people to think of black people as 'primitive'.

Buckingham argues that it is not possible to produce the definitive 'non-racist programme'. Referring to the very different responses he got from both white and black children, he suggests that 'racism' is a function of the interaction between audience and text, not an *inherent* property which texts either do or do not possess'. (Nevertheless programme makers are bound by the Race Relations Act not to broadcast material that could be 'an incitement to racial hatred', and racist jokes that could 'offend against good taste or decency' are not permitted under the IBA Television Programme Guidelines.) Buckingham argues that it is impossible to eradicate bias because everybody has assumptions about the world and about their own and other people's place in it, – and these will be embodied in the texts that people produce. He points out that the use of stereotypes is a useful means of classifying and making sense of the world and suggests that the appropriate way for teachers to deal with media racism is to teach children to detect and analyse sources of bias, both in themselves and in the material they study.

Of course, in the case of home-viewed programmes like *Blue Peter*, a teacher will not be at hand to point out the sub-texts of the programme's middle-class discourses. Children will have to work it out for themselves. In his essay *Black Blue Peter*, Bob Ferguson criticises *Blue Peter* for telling the story of Lee Boo, an 18th century Pacific island prince who came back to East London on an East India Company merchant ship, from the British point of view, rather than from a Pacific island point of view. The narrator is, apparently, wrong to say that the natives of the island 'looked a fearsome sight' to the crew of the British ship. It would have been more ideologically appropriate, in view of the East India Company's exploitation and cruelty in the Pacific, to say that the British ship looked a fearsome sight to the island natives.

Is *Blue Peter* being racist to tell the story in this form? In its defence, it needs to be said that, if you are trying to get across historical information to a very large, mixed-ability audience of six- to 12-year-olds, it probably makes sense to start from a British child's point of view. How would it have appealed to its audience if they had told the story as a tale of the British corrupting the innocence of the Pacific islanders? In the first place, it does not sound as if such a treatment would have been historically relevant in this particular case. Prince Lee Boo doesn't seem to have minded being brought to Britain. In the second place, the reaction of the British crew to the 'fearsome-looking' Pacific islanders would almost certainly have been shared by any British child, black or white, making the same trip for the first time. A black child brought up in Brixton or Handsworth or St Paul's is unlikely to identify with an 18th century Pacific islander; he or she would be more likely to identify with the apprehensive sailors from London (just as the West Indian Londoners objected to Africans being shown as representative of black people generally). There is a good case for arguing that *Blue Peter*, given the limitations imposed by the youthfulness and Britishness of its audience, was right to take as its starting point for this story, the audience's own point of view, limited though it may (temporarily) be.

Cultural identity

This raises the difficult question of cultural identity underlying the anxieties expressed about racial depictions in the media. What exactly is the cultural identity of a black child growing up in a British city and how should television reflect this? The young black British comedian, Lenny Henry, used to joke: 'Enoch Powell wants to give us £1,000 to go home – that's cool. It's only £10 on the train from here to Birmingham.' Questions are frequently raised about how often, and in what manner, black people are represented on television, and whether this representation is fair. About 4 per cent of the UK population of 54 million is non-white: 2

107

per cent Asian, 1 per cent Afro-Caribbean (half born in the UK) and the rest mixed or of other races, such as Chinese and Arab. Over half the Afro-Caribbeans live in London and comprise 10 per cent of the population of inner London. Black Afro-Caribbeans are much less widely represented as part of the population in other areas of the country. They constitute 3 per cent of the population of the West Midlands and smaller proportions of one or two other metropolitan areas. Asians are also concentrated in London and in industrial areas of Yorkshire, Lancashire and the Midlands. There are thus large parts of the country, including areas of urban deprivation, such as some cities in Scotland and Northern Ireland, where non-white people are hardly seen at all, and others where they seem to be very numerous. Should depiction of the races on television reflect these distributions? Should black characters be more frequent and prominent than they might be in the population as a whole, in the interests of promoting racial harmony? Should black people be depicted as having a separate culture from that of the white British, or should they be shown as being no different from the whites? Should there be 'integrated casting' with black actors playing any part in a drama, regardless of colour? What do black people themselves want?

In a survey of over 1000 Afro-Caribbeans aged 16 and over carried out for the BBC's Broadcasting Research Department in 1986 (from which the above figures come), it was found that black people as a whole watch less television than the average for the UK population. Young blacks watched more TV than young whites, whereas older black people did not watch nearly as much TV as older white people. This could suggest that many black people, certainly among the older generation, are voting with their switches. Both blacks and whites expressed almost identical levels of satisfaction (or dissatisfaction) with programmes. Nevertheless, when opinions about individual programmes were asked for, black people generally rated them lower than did white people.

This survey also asked black people how much they felt they 'belonged' to the UK: 22 per cent said they felt they always belonged; 39 per cent sometimes belonged; 32 per cent said they felt they never belonged. Seven per cent didn't know or didn't answer. The equivalent responses for UK viewers as a whole were 78 per cent, 15 per cent, 4 per cent and 3 per cent. From this study it's clear that many black people do feel alienated from British society. The survey did not talk to children – but people who were born in Britain were much more likely (29 per cent) to say they 'always' belonged than people not born in Britain (16 per cent). This survey found that the more people felt they belonged in the UK, the more likely they were to say they watched TV regularly and that they liked the programmes. The researchers concluded from their results that 'alienation reduces the extent to which an individual can participate in the cultural activities of the society in which he/she lives'. In other words, people who feel they don't belong in a community are less likely to join in its popular leisure activities like watching television.

The finding that young people born in the UK watched more television, and were also more likely to feel that they belonged, suggests that alienation may not be 'caused' by television; it may be something that older viewers themselves already feel because of the difference between the society reflected in TV programmes and the one they grew up in, or would like to live in. Such feelings are less likely to be experienced by children growing up in Britain, but they are unlikely to be absent altogether. This may be particularly true of the Asian community which has been very successful in preserving much of its culture, religion and language intact in the transfer from India and Pakistan to Britain. An attempt to chronicle the effects of such a transfer was made in a BBC pre-school programme, made in 1986, called *What's Inside?*, which was about a correspondence between an Anglo-Indian child in England and her grandfather in India; it was introduced by Floella Benjamin, a very popular black presenter.

It would have been useful to know what the impact of this programme was on very young children, but there is at least some information about the reactions of older children; some BBC audience research on seven- to 13-year-olds found that the majority of them did not watch the programme. Of those that did, 21 per cent liked the stories 'very much' and 48 per cent liked them 'a little'. The majority of children (86 per cent) liked Floella Benjamin and the younger children tended to rate the programme more highly than the older ones.

Although this was a small sample (probably due to the fact that seven- to 13-year-olds are often not at home from school by 4pm when the programme was shown), it shows a positive response to the stories, and to the personality of the presenter, which might well have been more positive had much younger children been surveyed. It is impossible to know, in surveys like these, whether children who didn't watch, or didn't like, the programme are simply not keen on the rather slow and 'babyish' pace of such simple stories, or because they don't like the fact that the story is about an Indian family. It would have been very helpful to have some more in-depth research into the children's opinions.

There have been many surveys, books and articles expressing the opinions of black adults about racism in the media (see, for example, *It Ain't Half Racist, Mum* edited by Phil Cohen and Carl Gardner) but there have been far fewer seeking or expressing the opinions and feelings of children on this subject. In fact, it can be quite difficult to find these because many researchers object to including questions about a child's ethnic background in questionnaires and children may quite reasonably object to giving this information. This obviously reflects a distrust about how the information may be used, based on fears of racial discrimination – but it makes research into the true attitudes and tastes of black children difficult. In nearly all the research I have quoted in this book, about children's tastes, learning abilities, attitudes and viewing habits, no distinctions have been made by any of the researchers between white and black children (with the exception of the research on *Sesame Street*).

As I write, probably the most popular (and certainly one of the most accomplished) comic performers in Britain is Lenny Henry, a comedian of West Indian origin from Dudley in Warwickshire, who began his television career on a children's programme, ITV's *Tiswas*. It is impossible for a white person like me to understand completely what it means to be black in a dominant white society. But, for us – as a white British family, concerned about racism, and with black friends – we feel that Henry's style and success is a breakthrough in terms of undermining racism. For our children, it is also more effective than the humour of black American comics, like Bill Cosby. The Cosby family could be any wealthy, middle-class, maddeningly attractive and folksy clan – funny, cute and apolitical.

The wealth and charm of the Cosbys, are, for many black people (as, for example, those who appeared in a discussion about media racism on the BBC's *Network* in June 1988) important in raising the dignity of the televised image of blacks. But other black contributors to this programme felt that Lenny Henry is more effective in terms of attacking racism, because his comedy is about *being* black. He doesn't ignore his black British ethnic background – he revels in it. Through characters like Delbert Wilkins, the streetwise DJ from Brixton, and Deekus, the elderly Jamaican reminiscing about discrimination in the Fifties over a pint of Guinness, Henry can make sharp and topical points about police harassment and white ignorance which nobody else has yet dared to make on mainstream British television – and can attract huge audiences, including children and young people, for them. Perhaps it will not be long before his example will, in his own words, produce 'a hip Asian comedian next, somebody who's a bit sussed out. They're all around waiting for the chance.'

Attitudes to gender

Another area of acute concern to do with children's attitudes is television's representation of the sexes. Studies of television content, carried out both in the United States and in Britain, over many years, show that, despite the efforts of the women's liberation movement, men continue to appear much more frequently than women on television, they are more likely to have active and authoritative roles, both in drama and in non-fiction programmes, they are more likely to appear even when elderly or unattractive, and they are more likely to be considered as experts. For example, in one study of television advertising in the United States, published in the *International Journal of Women's Studies* in 1981, it was found that 90 per cent of voice-overs in advertisements were male. When characters were shown demonstrating or using the advertised products, over 80 per cent of female characters were shown in the home, while nearly 70 per cent of male characters were shown at work, in business or management. At around the same time a British study, 'Sex role stereotyping in British television advertisements', found even worse stereotyping in a week's commercials shown in the North West ITV region. Women, as in the US, performed their usual domestic function of using the products – but when it came to putting forward arguments in favour of the product, only 37 per cent of British female characters were allowed to do this, whereas 70 per cent of American female characters did. Women on TV commercials were to be seen and not heard.

In *Children's Television Commercials: A Content Analysis*, a study carried out in the 1970s, the authors found that boys appeared more often than girls and that girls were more likely to be shown in adverts for food, games and dolls, while boys were more likely to be shown playing outdoors with active toys such as games, toy cars and planes. Girls played housewifely roles, boys pretended to be soldiers or racing drivers. An analysis of children's programmes, too, showed that male characters occurred far more frequently in all kinds of programmes, including cartoons (they outnumbered females by three to one during the week and four to one at weekends). How does this affect children's views both of the sex roles appropriate to themselves and of the sex roles in the adult world? Do the stereotyped portrayals of the sexes reflect the reality of how the sexes really behave? And if they do, (after all, both research and experience show that domestic chores *are* primarily carried out by women and girls, and that most top jobs *are* held by men), should television portrayals be used to try and redress these imbalances?

Children's views

Studies done in both America and Britain show that right from the pre-school stage, children prefer presenters and characters on television of their own sex; girls like females, boys like males. In a survey carried out by the BBC in 1985, it was found that girls identified far more strongly with, and thought more highly of, female presenters and boys felt the same about male presenters. The authors of this study suggest that, since girls between four and 15 constitute 49 per cent of the child audience, they are not being fairly treated. Of the children's programmes covered by the survey, only three had female presenters, whereas there were 14 men. There were no programmes presented only by a woman and in six programmes there were no women presenters at all. Research reported by Barrie Gunter in his book *Television and Sex Role Stereotyping* found some differences in the pattern of girls/females and boys/males identifications. In studies looking at children's learning from factual programmes, such as news, both boys and girls learned more from a male presenter than a female one, and boys learned more than girls. Girls were particularly bad at remembering what the female newscaster had said. It seems as if girls have particular difficulty accepting people of their own sex in authoritative·roles – a problem which boys suffer from less.

This apparently greater flexibility among boys was borne out by one of the studies showing two TV characters, male and female, behaving both in 'normal' and in counter-stereotyped ways (a man being gentle and a woman being assertive). For boys the more stereotypical (i.e. assertive) the man was, the more they liked him; the more counter-stereotypical the female was (i.e. also assertive), the more they liked her. Girls did not respond in this way. Generally, the role in which a man behaves in a 'feminine' way was the least liked by either sex. It seems that both boys and girls, but particularly boys, like television characters when they behave in ways which are considered to be masculine, whereas feminine-type behaviour, particularly in men, is not so appealing. Research such as this suggests that children already have quite firm views about what is and is not appropriate behaviour for people of different sexes, and television may have quite a difficult job shifting these views.

This is not to say that television should not try. Stereo-types may reflect, particularly for children whose experience of life is limited, the reality of the way sex roles are usually allocated in society – but these roles are never the whole story. Many children themselves experience the repressive-ness of adult expectations about how boys and girls should or should not behave, and suffer from them. I remember seeing the disappointment on a two-year-old boy's face when his mother told him to get off a pink My Little Pony ride-along toy at a toddlers' club, because 'that toy's for little girls, not for you'. One Sunday afternoon, I took Elinor and her friend Nicola, then aged seven and eight, to Connaught Water in Epping Forest, where they had the time of their lives building dams and getting covered in mud and dirty water. I watched small girl after small girl, dressed in pretty dresses and white socks, walk wistfully by on their Sunday outings with the family, looking enviously at the two urchins. Some boys do like playing with dolls and many girls love getting dirty and building dams; television could do much to 'legitimise' these minority tastes (if, indeed, they are minority.) There is no need for the leader of the gang or the computer expert, in the story, always to be a boy. There is no need for the sensible one who makes the sandwiches, or who minds the younger children, always to be a girl. The same is true of advertising. Showing children behaving in traditionally stereotyped ways cannot always be justified as social realism, expected by children; it is just as likely to be simple laziness and lack of imagination on the part of the programme and commercial makers. As such, there is no excuse for it.

Where children's programmes do show counter-stereotypical characters, the effects on children can be encouraging. In a study for the IBA carried out by British psychologist Kevin Durkin in 1983, an edition of the pre-school programme *Rainbow* was shown to 52 primary school children. The programme told the story of a family where the father was made redundant and the mother had to go out to work; the father stayed at home doing the household chores. A week before the programme the children were given a questionnaire about different occupations: 'male' ones, such as bus driver, doctor, farm worker, and 'female' ones such as nurse, shop assistant and so on. They were also asked about domestic activities – DIY, cooking, cleaning and so on. They were asked whether a man, a woman or both men and women could carry out these tasks. After they'd seen *Rainbow* they were tested again, and both boys and girls showed a marked change away from stereotyped views of sex roles. They were much more likely to say that women could perform 'male' tasks and vice versa after seeing the programme. (Control groups who saw a different programme or no programme did not show the same change of attitude.) Durkin did not have so much luck with another study with adolescents, in which they were asked to rate prospective occupations as male or female. A film about counter-stereotyped career choices made no impression on either boys' or girls' views about which jobs would be appropriate for them.

Views about sex roles obviously come from a variety of sources, not just television. It is unlikely that, even if television bombarded its audience with images of caring men and assertive women all the time, that this would overcome other pressures to conform with traditional sex role expectations. Peer groups, families, personality, schooling, life's experiences, physical attributes, will all affect how a child perceives and enacts his or her sex role. Kevin Durkin, in his book *Television Sex Roles and Children* makes an important point about the different impacts of stereotyped and counter-stereotyped portrayals on television:

> Evidence that viewing counter-stereotyped material can lead to changes in children's attitudes is *not* in itself evidence that viewing traditional sex stereotyped material has led to the establishment of these attitudes in the first place . . . TV sex role stereotypes . . . are broadly consistent with a host of other potential influences . . . (which) are occurring throughout the child's social life most of the time. A counter-stereotyped message, on the other hand, *contradicts* the normal flow of information and behaviour, and thus offers a radically different learning experience.

Thus, the 'good news' about television and its influence on children's perceptions of gender roles is rather mixed. In a sense, it is bad news in that other cultural influences are so strong that counter-stereotypical efforts may not be able to shift these influences. The evidence from the *Rainbow* study, however, suggests that the younger the age at which counter-stereotypes are presented to children, the more acceptable they are likely to be. On the other hand, the news is good in that research suggests that television does not have nearly such a powerful influence on attitudes as many people would like to believe. There is a strong case for saying that young children should be exposed to as many different options and possibilities about their future lives as possible, and that this is an educational, social and moral imperative regardless of whether or not it produces 'good' (which may only be another word for 'fashionable') ideological development. The world is a rich and complex place. Children themselves are rich and complex people with many potential talents, whether they are white or black, male or female. Television will be 'good' for children to the extent that it reflects the richness, diversity and complexity of the world and of human experience – not to the extent to which it reflects approved ideologies.

The girls' gang in our street is currently very taken with the film *Annie*, which they had seen on video during the school holidays. The film has some rather heavy-handed ideology about millionaires and 'the American dream', but it is primarily about a group of resilient orphan girls, and how they triumph over adult ill-treatment and corruption. It focuses in particular on the spunky and appealing Annie. When Annie finally escapes from her captors, through her own intelligence and daring, an adult character articulates the moral which, unlike references to 'the American way', is apparently the most meaningful aspect of the story for children: 'A child without courage is like a night without stars.' Stories and programmes which encourage children to believe in their own strength and potential will be most likely to enable them, when the time comes, to adopt the appropriate ideologies for themselves.

8 | Television in the classroom

A teacher I met during preparation of this book, who uses schools television programmes very imaginatively in her infants' class teaching, spoke dismissively of the way children viewed television at home: 'It's mindless, really. They go home, turn it on and it's just something to occupy them.' This comment suggests that, for some teachers, little has changed since the 1973 study of teachers' attitudes to television, *Mass Media and the Secondary School*. This revealed that popular television was considered by most teachers to be irrelevant to the classroom and was never discussed. The research also found that, where teachers did talk about television, it was with the feeling that they had a duty to protect children against its harmful effects. There were anxieties, too, about TV's effects on children's verbal and imaginative ability and there was a widespread lack of knowledge among teachers about the sorts of programmes that children habitually watched. Yet many teachers use TV in school for teaching purposes.

Is there really such a difference between television watched in school and television watched at home? It is worth asking why television should be an acceptable medium for conveying information about history, geography, maths, science, languages and literature and not an acceptable medium when it is used for leisure. We do not make this distinction with books: teachers clearly accept that novels, which may be read to while away a train journey or to relax after work, are also a legitimate topic for academic study. There seems no reason why television cannot be used in this way too, particularly as it is such a pervasive medium. The programmes made for study purposes also use many of the same techniques as those used by entertainment programmes – such as narrative episodes, rapid editing, disembodied voice-overs, intercutting to suggest simultaneity of action, various kinds of camera movements and angles to create different points of view or emphasis. If children were not familiar with these techniques from their own televiewing, would they be able to make as much sense of schools television as is required?

This chapter will look at some of the ways television is used in the classroom. Obviously this includes programmes made specifically for teachers to use, produced by the Schools and Education Departments of the BBC and ITV, with detailed teachers' notes and printed back-up for children. But it also includes ways in which the television which children watch at home can become part of the educational process. Television in the classroom is not only about television as a teaching tool: it is also about the less common, but increasing, use of television as a teaching topic.

Schools television

The first use of television – as a tool – is very widely accepted in this country's schools – a 1987 survey of listening and viewing in over 800 UK schools carried out by the BBC revealed that 98 per cent of primary schools and 99 per cent of secondary schools had at least one colour TV (the average number of TVs in secondary schools was five). Virtually all secondary schools and 78 per cent of primary schools had a video recorder, which meant that programmes could be recorded for use at the teacher's own convenience, and need not be seen only at transmission times. The use of the video also allows teachers to use programmes in a greater variety of ways – for instance, stopping the tape at a

119

key moment and discussing it with the class, or playing back the tape to emphasise a point. Some schools programmes are now made in sections, with this possibility in mind. The video also enables teachers to preview programmes, so that they can prepare lessons based on them or so that they can check on controversial material.

Schools programmes are provided both by the BBC and Independent Television, with protected blocks of airtime during the day in term-time on BBC2 and Channel 4 respectively. They range from programmes for under-fives, like the BBC's *You and Me*, through programmes like *Watch* and *Zig Zag* (general knowledge) aimed at infant school and lower junior children and ITV's *Junior Maths*, through to very specialised language, science and history programmes for secondary school exam candidates. Schools programmes have pioneered controversial topics like sex education and sensitive social issues such as AIDS and homosexuality (both treated in the 1987/88 series of the BBC's *Scene*, aimed at 14- to 16-year-olds). Some of the drama made by schools departments has been of such a high standard that it has been shown during main transmission times in the evening. A recent adventurous innovation was a spin-off from Channel 4's soap opera *Brookside*, which was shown as a schools programme, *South*, and featured the problems of young unemployed people from Liverpool, finding work and accommodation in London. This was a bold step, in that it acknowledged the existence of 'entertainment' programmes as a source of serious educational material: watching *Brookside* for the teachers and pupils who viewed *South* could not be dismissed as entirely 'mindless'.

Viewing in the classroom

Watching television in the classroom is a very different experience from watching it at home. Much of the research on the 'effects' of television, and on what people learn from particular programmes, is divorced from the context of actual viewing. I was interested to find out how a schools programme was used in a real school and I selected one of the most enduringly popular of schools programmes, the BBC's *Watch*. This 'miscellany' programme, aimed at 'widening the experience' of four- to seven-year-olds, has now been going for 21 years and is taken by around 70 per cent of British primary schools. It covers a wide range of topics, grouped into themes such as autumn, summer, the elements and entertainment. Frank Flynn, Education Officer at the BBC Schools' Department, explains that *Watch* fits very naturally into the cross-curricular approaches to learning used by primary school teachers. 'Most of current infant practice is topic-based, aimed at integration. One programme of *Watch* can generate language work, geography, history, science.'

The themes and topics of *Watch*, as with other schools programmes, arise out of regular discussions between producers, education officers, teachers and children around the country, both before and after transmissions. Both BBC and ITV use their education officers to advise and follow up on their educational output. As already mentioned, attractive publications and teachers' notes accompany programmes. Schools television is thus an example of how television can be produced, and viewed, not in isolation from other contexts, but with continual co-operation and feedback between producers and users.

In a programme like *Watch*, the television medium enables a variety of teaching techniques to be used, which will appeal to children of different tastes and abilities: stories, animations, drama, film and music can be particularly valuable in making the past, or remote parts of the world, accessible. Such a mixture of techniques enables schools programmes to be enjoyed by many pre-school children at home, even though some of the content may be outside their range of experience. An experienced infant teacher, Diane Lewis, Deputy Head of Brooklands School in North London, values what schools television offers her pupils: 'For a subject like natural history, television can do more in ten minutes than we can do in two weeks.'

Like most teachers who use television for teaching purposes, she emphasises the importance both of follow-up and of preparation in consolidating the information given in the programme. I went to see *Watch* with Diane's class of top infants, both to observe how they watched the programme, and to see how their teacher followed it up in the classroom.

Watching *Watch*

Watch is a highlight of Tuesday mornings for Diane Lewis' class of 29 top infant boys and girls (aged six and seven). They watch it in their dining hall, ranged around the room, sitting wherever they like. Obviously friends choose to sit together, which enables them to nudge each other or comment on interesting aspects of the programme. While the programme was being shown, on the day of my visit, the children behaved like an attentive audience; they sat still and, on the whole, quiet, with an awareness of, and sensitivity to, the fact that if they fidgeted or chattered other people's concentration would be disturbed. Viewing television in this kind of 'audience' situation is obviously very different from viewing at home. Research shows (see Chapter 9) that, at home, viewing can be a much more casual business, intermixed with other activities, and with lots of talking and comment. When children watch in a group, the programme becomes, in Frank Flynn's words, 'a shared experience. At home, older brothers and sisters can cow or dominate. At school, they're with their peers.'

Watching TV with peers also increases co-operative audience behaviour, and reaction. Children are more likely to laugh, cheer, boo, and applaud when they are in a large viewing group. I once saw a class of six-year-olds rise to their

122

feet and clap at the end of a particularly ingenious *You and Me* animation, a reaction I have never seen from children watching the programme at home. Diane Lewis's children did occasionally comment casually on this *Watch* programme (called 'Under the Earth') but in general they behaved as if they knew that the purpose of the transmission was to teach them things and that their task was to listen and view attentively.

The programme lasted 20 minutes and was in two main sections: the first showed a visit to a mining museum in Wales, a disused coal mine, and also included some film of still-working coal mines, thus touching on the topic of energy and fuel. The second part was about how coal was formed and thus moved from recent history to pre-history, with animated reconstructions of primeval forests being compressed into fossil fuel. The topic of animal and leaf fossils was also demonstrated. Certain points of the programme brought out some spontaneous unison behaviour in the class: there was a countdown from 12 to one at the beginning, in which they all joined. When the presenter asked a question: 'What do we use coal for?', everybody shouted 'Fire'. Visually striking images, such as a necklace made of crystal and a close-up of a fossilised leaf in a rock, produced gasps of appreciation. At the historical fact that children as young as six or seven (their own age) used to work in mines, there were gasps of horror. There were a number of individual comments, such as 'Cor, look! Lovely!' as the cage carrying the visitors to the mine descended and much appreciation (such as laughter or leaning forward) of the drilling process shown in the modern coal-mine. The children's reactions suggested that they were paying close attention to both the visuals and the soundtrack of the programme and that it was providing them with information that they found unusual and fascinating. As they went back to their class, there was a lively hum of discussion.

The classroom discussion, led by the children's teacher, that followed the viewing, was not entirely typical of usual follow-up work, since it was for my benefit – we wanted to elicit verbally as much as possible of what the children had learned from the programme and what they thought of it. There was no immediate opportunity for practical or individual work. Nevertheless, the discussion gave some clear examples of how a programme like this one can stimulate work in a number of subject areas, how it can encourage children to relate what they are learning to their own experience, and how it can generate empathy. One little girl, talking about the thought of children working in the mines, said to her teacher: 'When you said "Can you imagine the children?", it was too horrible for me to imagine' – and she squeezed her eyes shut. She obviously was imagining it and finding it disturbing.

One of the most striking aspects of the discussion was the ease with which children were able to relate aspects of the programme to other relevant topics and experiences, without having to be prompted by the teacher. Seeing the experience of the programme participants 'under the earth' prompted vivid reminiscences. One child had actually visited the same Welsh mining museum: 'It was cold. It smelt like thin air, cold, old air. It was dirty and dusty. I liked the lift but we had to move to one side because the wet was coming down on us. You come out of there with awful dirty trousers.'

Another child had visited a similar mining museum, but her memories were not of atmosphere, but of human reactions: 'When we got out of the lift, my little brother kept running around. He cuddled me, he was really scared. He kept losing mummy's and daddy's hand and we couldn't see very well. It was scary.' A boy was able to extend the underground theme to an experience that had not been featured in the programme at all – but was obviously relevant: 'I went into a place where there were rocks hanging down and there were sculptures like people; they were made out of water. That was under the ground.' The teacher asked if anyone knew the name of the 'sculptures made out of water', and nobody did. So the class was given the task of finding out.

History was touched on in the discussion, with references to the steam age and what London used to be like when smoke from coal-fired chimneys created the great smogs; one child had a coal fire, but, for most, coal belonged to an unfamiliar past. The nearest one boy could get to it was saying that he had plastic coal on his model railway train. Geological aspects caught the children's interest most, perhaps because rocks, stones, fossils and charcoal were most directly related to their own experience. One observant child pointed out that there was a fossil holding open the door of one of the junior classrooms. A lively debate arose about why coal was black when it had originally been made out of green and brown trees. Again, the challenge was given to go and find out why this was so. One ingenious child suggested that it might be like 'the way colours in a paint-tray always ended up black when you mixed them together'.

The plight of both ponies and children in dark and dangerous mines aroused sympathy and concern. One child promised to bring in a video she had about a pit pony, called *Escape from the Dark*. Again, an unprompted analogy was drawn between the information in the programme and other historical information that one child already knew about: 'Young children used to have to work a lot and if they were naughty, when they found the country of Australia they sent them over there.' A child who had been to Australia said she had seen the boats the children travelled in: 'They were really tiny and they had to sleep on this hard stuff.' Much of the children's knowledge came from their own direct experience, but an interesting example occurred of how they used television at home as a source of information about the world and were able to relate it to the geological information in *Watch*: 'On *Newsround* there was a statue in Australia . . .' 'No, Egypt!' '. . . and it was made of limestone and it was all crumbling and the shoulder fell off.' Virtually all the children had seen this item and were able to supply missing details to the child who was the main narrator. The teacher made use of this to ask the statue's name (the Sphinx) and when it had been made, and why it was crumbling (because of pollution). Because she had not seen the programme herself, the children were able to take on the roles of explicator and narrator. This was something they obviously enjoyed and is an example of how TV viewed at home can be put to positive use in the classroom.

Although this was not a typical teaching session in terms of follow-up to the programme, because the children didn't have much opportunity to work individually, the discussion was enlightening. It was also a valuable exercise in co-operative interchange, lightly 'chaired' by the teacher. Every child had a chance to say something and to reveal some unique piece of information or insight. The discussion revealed that the knowledge in the programme had been well assimilated, particularly to the extent that the children were able to relate it to knowledge they already had. Their ability to describe their experiences, to imagine other lives and times, to take turns and to listen and respond to others was very evident from the session. What happened with these children watching at school was, in some respects, different from the situation of viewing at home, because they knew they had to listen and attend to the programme; they knew they were going to be 'tested' afterwards, and they were watching in a group, which promoted rather different behaviour from the behaviour of a child relaxing in her own living room. Nevertheless, if children can pick up so much from one short schools programme, and relate it so articulately to other areas of knowledge and experience at the ages of six and seven, it seems unlikely that this ability to learn and imagine is switched off when they watch television at home. The fact that the teacher had watched with them, and was able to stimulate and share in the discussion, also showed how much an interested adult can contribute to children's experience of watching television.

Media studies

In the United Kingdom, media studies – that is, the study of television and other mass media, such as newspapers and advertising – has fairly recently become an accepted subject in secondary schools, both for GCSE and A Level exams, and as an option within the TVEI (Technical and Vocational Education Initiative) programme. It may well be threatened by the introduction of the national curriculum, as are other subjects considered to be non-essential, such as drama and sociology – both, interestingly, subjects concerned with teaching children about themselves and other people and how they do, or might, or ought to, behave and express themselves. Given the concern so often expressed by political leaders about the moral effects of the mass media, the marginalising of subjects which directly address issues of human behaviour and judgement seems perverse.

However, it may well be that the study of the media will survive within the shelter of other subjects and as a cross-curricular discipline, which can be used in science, in the humanities, in art, and in technical subjects. At the moment, media studies in this country are conducted primarily by teachers of English, and concentrate particularly on critical analysis. The aims of media studies ought to be, in the words of David Lusted of the British Film Institute's Education Department, 'the acquisition and use of practices of production and skills of analysis', rather than what he calls 'fault-finding, the picking of holes in television'. This approach emphasises the cross-curricular usefulness of media studies as the promotion of a general set of intellectual skills. There is also a growth in media education in primary schools, the aims of which are currently being considered by a joint BFI/DES working party and set forth in a series of Working Papers.

In the book in which Lusted's essay appears, *TV and Schooling*, a number of people give their views on why and how the media should be taught in schools. Much of the material was prompted by a Department of Education report called *Popular TV and Schoolchildren* written by a group of teachers in 1983. The concern of teachers, as expressed in this report, is similar to the concerns expressed above: 'It is based on both awareness of their [the mass media's] potential as educational tools and anxiety lest they be negative influences on the attitudes and behaviour of young people.' Again, the concern with 'negative influences' rather than positive ones is characteristic of much adult comment on children's televiewing, as is the emphasis on the value of education, as distinct from leisure, culture and entertainment. Other contributors to the book show different concerns, such as the need for children to understand the structural, political and economic realities of broadcasting; to be aware of 'biases', or sources of bias; to understand the realities of the production process (this is a plea from a producer); and an understanding of the nature of 'entertainment' – is it mere escapism (and does that matter), or is it something more? At secondary level, agreed syllabuses, incorporating many of these topics, are being used in schools. How media education may affect the students in terms of their future attitudes to mass communications – will the readership of the mass tabloid press decline, while quality readership rises? – remains to be seen.

At the primary level, educationists are still working towards what media education ought to be about and how it can be applied in practice. In the most recent of the BFI/DES Working Papers (1988), one writer claims that 'there appear to be many misconceptions as to whether it [media education] involves learning to master media technologies or using the media as a focus for project work'. One primary school project, outlined in an earlier Working Paper (1987), suggests that it can be both. In this project, a class of nine- and ten-year-olds first of all studied the techniques of advertising, discussed and wrote about their own favourite adverts, and found out about how adverts 'target' particular groups in the audience. They then made some advertisements of their own. The aim of the campaign was to promote two kinds of biscuit: Chew Chew Chocs for eight- to 11-year-olds, and Star Biscuits for five- to seven-year-olds. (The project should have included baking the biscuits, but there wasn't enough time!) All creative stages were included – pictorial story boards, scripts, music, packaging and videotaping.

Below is part of the Star Biscuits song, performed by two boys, with group backing:

> *Boys* We have just thought of something to eat . . .
> *Group* Star biscuits ooo wa bu da ba [*twice*]
> *Boys* We have to hide so that you don't take our . . .
> *Group* Star biscuits . . . *etc*
> *Boys* We have come out to play 'cause we have finished our . . .
> *Group* Star biscuits . . . *etc*
> *Boys* We have to go back in to get some more . . .
> *Group* Star biscuits . . . *etc*

The commercial ended with a close-up of the packet (also designed by the children), a caption and voice-over saying: 'Star biscuits are very healthy. They also have few additives. They are low in sugar with natural flavouring.'

The teachers responsible for this project, Peter Hart and Fiona Collins from Christchurch Primary School, felt that it 'provided for the children a more concrete and direct means of access to media concepts related to advertising than more conventional teaching methods could have'. They also pointed out that the activities involved work in music, mathematics, art and design – a truly cross-curricular approach. They were also pleased with the children's language work, and with the extent to which the children were able to see that their commercials had a persuasive purpose and were thus not entirely 'truthful'. The pupils realised that if they had been making a public health video about the dangers of biscuit eating, the ideas would have been presented differently – that 'representations will vary according to the purposes and intentions of whoever is producing the piece of media'.

Teaching through television

Although many claims are made for the value of media education in this country, and, as described above, some valuable work is being done in UK schools, when it comes to the systematic evaluation of the usefulness of 'teaching television', we have to turn to the United States. In her book *Mind and Media*, Patricia Marks Greenfield describes a number of US research projects demonstrating how the skills of television viewing can be both taught, and extended to other areas of learning. In one study, a teacher, Rosemary Lehman, taught her eight- and nine-year-old children about the codes and aesthetics of television, in a way similar to the way style and technique are taught in literature classes. This was part of her regular practice, but, for the purposes of research, her class was studied for a year and a comparison was made with a similar class of the same age, taught by the same teacher, but without using the television curriculum. The 'television class' was taught about techniques such as light, shadow, colour, forms, motion and time/space. Pupils were encouraged to observe when motion was determined by camera movement and when by the movement of people, and when they coincided. They were also encouraged to look at how TV deals with time: how much time has really passed, in terms of the duration of the programme, compared with how much time passed in the programme. They learned to see how editing can 'collapse' time. These children were thus taught to see the difference between reality and television, not only in terms of content, but also in terms of form: real time is not the same as edited TV time.

At the end of the year, children from both groups were asked to write about a short piece of television. The children from the TV class were much more likely to comment on the forms and style of the programme – the colour, the composition of shots and so on. This increased critical awareness was not confined to the television teaching exercises they had been given in class. It improved their critical judgements generally. The other group wrote only about storyline. This is the utilisation of 'modality' markers, as described by Bob Hodge and David Tripp, and mentioned in Chapter 5. Being able to see how a programme is made makes it much more possible for children to preserve the distinction between reality and fantasy. As happened with the TV class in this study, children need to be given a critical vocabulary for describing the forms of television – it may be that they can only describe storylines, because they lack the technical knowledge to be able to refer to 'changes of shot', 'panning', 'zooming' and so on.

A particularly interesting side-effect of the project was that it had a spin-off on children's televiewing habits at home. In Greenfield's words, 'action and formula programs dropped from their lists of favorite shows and were replaced by more challenging programs'. *Charlie's Angels* dropped from first to tenth place at the end of the year, and whereas no documentaries or documentary dramas were in the list at the beginning of the year, *Holocaust* appeared in the list at the end. Of course, one would expect children's television tastes to change over a year. And when a highly publicised and controversial series like *Holocaust* is shown, it might not be surprising if children watch it. But the key evidence that the change in children's tastes from the easy to the more discriminating, was due to their TV lessons, was what happened to the non-TV group. They, too, had matured by a year and had been exposed to the *Holocaust* publicity. But no comparable shift in their viewing tastes occurred. The use of this control group points to the value of controlled research in attempting to establish the value, or otherwise, of any new educational initiative, such as media studies. Such an approach would be very valuable in this country, which is on the point of so many curricular changes.

My doctoral research suggested that people do 'notice' techniques like cuts and close-ups, but that this is rarely conscious. Cuts and close-ups appear to have an effect on the way people later remember and describe what they have seen and heard on TV – they are used as a kind of a 'grammar'. But, just as many people are unable to articulate their own spoken grammar (even though they use it absolutely correctly), so many television viewers will not be consciously and critically aware of the 'grammar' and the techniques of TV, unless these are taught. Rosemary Lehman's children who could only write about storylines, were only eight and nine, but in a research project carried out at the North East London Polytechnic in which I was involved, a similar lack of formal TV awareness was demonstrated by teenagers. This study, reported in the *Times Educational Supplement* (29 April 1988), tested teenagers' responses to a schools TV programme about AIDS. When asked what they liked or disliked about the programme, a high proportion of these 14- to 16-year-olds said that they liked the characters in the dramatised story, or that they didn't like how one character treated another. They could only think in terms of the storyline. Comparatively few mentioned stylistic aspects of the programme – the acting, or the script, or the production values. It would seem that this approach to TV does need to be taught.

Teaching critical skills

In another study described by Patricia Marks Greenfield, a junior school teacher, Sharon Neuwirth, noticed that children in her class were retelling televised stories with great attention to detail, but with little grasp of plot. They seemed incapable of reconstructing the sequence of events that made up a story. (This teacher was obviously not one who discouraged the discussion of popular television in her classroom.) Finding that the children had the same problem in discussing books and stories read in class, she thought she would teach plot comprehension through television. She decided that conflict of some kind was at the basis of all story structure – that characters had a problem to solve and that some obstacle stood in their way. She chose a beautifully simple way to introduce her pupils to this way of critically analysing texts. She asked them to watch anything they liked on TV at home (difficult to imagine in some British classrooms), and to be prepared to sum up the programme the next day in three sentences: Who was the show about? What did the main character want? What stood in his or her way?

When the children had successfully managed this, Sharon Neuwirth asked them to carry out the same tasks – of identifying conflicts – in other media: in film, school plays and short stories. Eventually, they were able to tackle long novels, because their difficulties in understanding plots which had prevented them from working their way through complex structures, had now been overcome. This teacher's approach was a wise one, because she started her students on their study of plots and stories using television – a medium with which they were all familiar and at home, and to which they all had easy access (not always the case with books). As Patricia Greenfield put it: 'Once concepts were learned in relation to this familiar medium, they could be transferred to more difficult and less familiar ones, notably print.'

Television exists in almost every home and in every school in the country. Yet its potential as an aid to learning, in the sense of skills acquisition, seems barely to be recognised. It would be gratifying to see teachers in the UK taking the positive line used by the American teachers described above, and using their students' obvious fascination with television as a starting point for learning, rather than something which has to be rejected and disapproved of. There are difficulties in introducing the study of television into an already pressurised curriculum – and many parents might be extremely concerned at the idea of their children studying *EastEnders* in school, as well as sitting slumped in front of it at home. But parents may not be the ideal sources of influence on children's televiewing habits, according to

Jerome and Dorothy Singer of Yale University. They found that it was easier to influence what children watched through teachers rather than through parents. But teachers need to be receptive to the idea that they *should* influence children's viewing, and that children are going to go on viewing whether teachers approve or not.

Every television viewing occasion is a potential source of learning about television, and hence about media forms generally. In the viewing of *Watch* that I described earlier, it would have been very instructive (although it would have required another visit) to ask the children to notice aspects of how the programme was made: which bits were in a studio, which were filmed, where was the camera when the presenters were down the mine, how it might have been possible to give this information without pictures, and so on. Children can learn a great deal of factual information from television – but the way television constructs messages and images is also a valuable teaching topic, and it arises every time a class group sits down in front of the set. If more use could be made of such opportunities, children watching television in the classroom could be learning not only about rocks, fossils, foreign lands and distant times (valuable though these are). They could also be learning critical and evaluative skills which would serve them well in every other area of educational life.

9 | Television as entertainment

In a paper given to the British Film Institute's Summer School on children and television in 1987, Professor William Melody, an expert on communications technology, repeatedly lamented the decline of children's programmes in the US that were 'of high quality and educational'. In linking 'high quality' with 'education', as distinct from entertainment, he expressed a very common belief about television – and about all forms of popular culture: that if something is to deserve the epithet of 'quality', it has to be in some sense didactic and 'improving'. Children, fortunately, have always been deeply resistant to this idea: every parent must have examples of lovingly crafted, expensive, wooden, 'educational' toys languishing at the bottom of the toy box, while the child plays with shocking-pink plastic gorillas from the cornflake packet. Nevertheless, many of us persist in trying to 'improve' our children through 'educational' activities, overlooking (and surely forgetting) that, for a child, the best toy, the best game, the best story and the best programme, is one that is fun.

The idea that fun is important and, indeed, probably essential to emotional and intellectual well-being, has always had to fight for respectability. Puritanism has a long tradition in Britain and in other English-speaking countries. Modern developmental psychologists as well as educationists are now at least convinced of the value of play in healthy development, and play has become a fruitful research area – one might almost say, a play area – for grown-ups. But one of the sad ironies of this recognition of the value of play, is that play can be in danger of becoming something that adults try to teach children to do, like making them eat their greens. It could be argued that the whole point of play is that it is something you want to do for the sheer fun of it, and sometimes because other people disapprove of it. By definition, it cannot be something that that you only do because someone says you ought to, and because it's good for you. Resistance to the idea that people should be able to do things solely because they enjoy them, even (especially) if they are 'bad' for them, seems to lie at the root of much of the prejudice against television: if so many people enjoy TV, it must be bad. And the programmes that people enjoy most, like soap opera or cartoons, must be the worst.

As mentioned in Chapter 4, similar resistance to cultural forms that were popular and entertaining in the past has been expressed throughout history, from Plato's suspicion of poetry onwards. In an essay on 'A History of Suspicion: Educational Attitudes to Television' in *TV and Schooling*, David Lusted quotes the *Edinburgh Review* of 1851 on the subject of the theatre:

> One powerful agent for the depraving of the boyish classes of our towns and cities is to be found in the cheap shows and theatres, which are so especially opened and arranged for the attraction and ensnaring of the young . . . it is not to be wondered at that the boy . . . becomes rapidly corrupted and demoralised and seeks to be the doer of the infamies which have interested him as a spectator.

How familiar this sounds. A BBC2 programme, *Television on Trial*, shown in November 1986, featured an American father who only allowed his children to watch television if it was showing opera, good drama (the 'depravity' of the theatre now being no longer a problem) or classical ballet. For any other programmes, they had to generate their own electricity by pedalling exercise bikes attached to a home-made dynamo. The message from this father to these children appeared to be: if you enjoy watching something, you've got to suffer for it. If it's something you wouldn't choose to watch, you can have it, as he put it, 'on the house'. This seems a quite effective way of putting children off high culture for life.

The values of 'showbiz'

In a highly critical article about TV in *New Internationalist* in February 1988, Joyce Nelson, author of *The Perfect Machine: TV in the Nuclear Age*, laments the neglect among American citizens of 'all the things a person is not doing during those seven hours they spend in front of the set each day'. (The unsubstantiated figure of seven hours per person is slipped in here, perhaps in the hope that nobody will wonder how the USA manages to feed, clothe, clean, house, transport, educate, defend, police and nurse itself, if everybody is watching television all day. For a more sceptical account of TV viewing figures, see Chapter 3.) This writer claims, again without quoting convincing evidence, that: 'It is the erosion – or elimination – of the imagination that is perhaps the most worrying aspect of TV's hidden curriculum.'

How Charles Dickens would have appreciated the irony of this remark. When he published his impassioned attack on utilitarian education in *Hard Times*, in 1854, it was the imagination (or 'fancy', as he called it) that was then seen as the enemy of childhood intellectual progress. Facts were what was required for a sound education. In *Hard Times*, young Cissie Jupe, her circus friends in 'the horse-riding', and the values of 'fancy', exoticism and humour that they represented, were considered by the teacher Thomas Gradgrind to be a thoroughly bad influence on respectable, middle-class children like his own. One cannot help feeling that, had critics like Joyce Nelson lived in Coketown, these critics would have been just as antipathetic to the circus, and its seduction of children away from more worthy activities, as they are to television now, despite their apparent championing of 'the imagination'. Not so Dickens. At the end of the novel, Cissie and Mr Sleary's circus become the saviours of the Gradgrind family, and it is clear that Dickens intended the colourful and unconventional 'showbiz' values of the circus to symbolise the integrity and warmth of basic human decency. We may feel, after 60 Oscar ceremonies, that 'showbiz' values have become slightly tawdry, but Dickens makes a convincing case. Unlike many critics of television (and, indeed, of the novel), Dickens was not a Puritan and lavishly celebrated vulgar pleasures in his books. His spirit is very much absent from the modern debate about television, which so often castigates the medium for being 'merely' entertaining, and only defends it when it is being 'educational'.

The following sections will look at some of the ways children use television as a leisure activity, and at the evidence which suggests that television programmes are not simply passively 'soaked up' by children, but are taken over by them and transformed in the other things that they do, so that television becomes part of their play (play in the widest sense, of being something you enjoy doing that you haven't been told to do). The relationship between television and other forms of childhood entertainment is sometimes seen as an unhealthy one, firstly, because TV watching is supposed to 'displace' more valuable activities (of which, more below), and secondly, because of the risks of commercial exploitation. However, it does not follow that, because a programme has commercial links with toys, books, songs or games, this makes it a bad programme. Indeed, such links provide a counter-argument to the 'displacement' theory, in that television programmes can actually encourage children to do other things, besides watching television.

Similarly, just because a toy is advertised on TV, this does not make it a bad toy. It seems unreasonable to assume that children's enjoyment of programmes, toys and other media is always uncritical – that they are the dupes of

Machiavellian producers and advertisers, without whose blandishments they would never want to buy 'rubbish' like plastic Thundercats, and would, instead, be reading great works of literature and building the Taj Mahal out of Meccano. There is simply no evidence for this view. Nor is there evidence that premature indulgence in media favoured by adults is likely to produce more competent and well-balanced adult personalities than does the kind of upbringing in which children are allowed to enjoy childish pleasures like reading comics, collecting garish toys, getting dirty and watching cartoons. Children who have been encouraged to enjoy media of their own choosing, no matter how banal these may seem to their elders, may be more eager to move on from *Beano*, Care Bears and *He-Man* to more demanding material as they mature, than will children who are never allowed to make their own choices. This self-directed approach to leisure would certainly be in line with current educational thinking and practice about how children learn. However, most long-term studies of children's development are concerned with health and educational performance, not with the effects of leisure-time activities on how they grow up. It would be useful to have such information.

Television's relationship with other activities

One of the most frequently recurring complaints about television is that it stops children from doing other things, which are assumed to be more important. As Joyce Nelson puts it in her claim that people are watching television for seven hours a day: 'A whole range of leisure pursuits, hobbies, social encounters, information sources are automatically excluded.' This argument not only assumes that all kinds of leisure pursuits, including vandalising the neighbourhood, are 'automatically' superior to watching television; it also (wrongly) assumes that other valuable activities are incompatible with it. As I have argued and, I hope, demonstrated, in earlier chapters of this book, television does not preclude other social and leisure activity. And when families are actually studied as they watch television (as described, for example, in David Morley's book, *Family Television: Cultural Power and Domestic Leisure*), it can be seen that the act of watching television –choosing channels, choosing programmes, timetabling viewing, discussing programme content – is very much a social activity, closely bound up with family dynamics. Television-viewing is an occasion which can be used by families in order to understand and sympathise with one another better (as in the example of Damon Grant's death in *Brookside* and its effect on our family, described in Chapter 6); it can also elicit different kinds of appreciative, co-operative audience behaviour in children, when they view it in a group, as at school (see Chapter 8). It can also generate follow-up activities, which might not otherwise have been engaged in (see Chapter 10).

The 'displacement' theory

Now that nearly every family has a TV set, it is difficult to know what children would have been doing, if they were not watching television. Any attempt to compare the behaviour of children in households with television, with the behaviour of children in households without television, immediately runs into the problem of not comparing like with like. The most that can be done is to compare children who watch very large amounts of television with children who watch less, taking as much account as possible of factors like social class, which can completely invalidate comparisons between light and heavy viewers, unless they are properly controlled for. For instance, it's no use saying that heavy television watchers do less well at school, if heavy television watchers come from a social group who have always done less well at school – the poor. Poorer people are much more likely to use television as a leisure activity, simply because they cannot afford to go out to the theatre, cinema or sporting occasions, or to buy books. If poor children don't do well in school, this cannot be attributed only to television. In her book, *Television and Children*, Aimée Dorr, a professor of education in Los Angeles, describes American research which suggests that children who watch more television do less well in school, but this is not a simple relationship. For lower class children, moderate amounts of viewing seem actually to improve their academic performance, but more than two or three hours a day is associated with poorer school performance, perhaps because, as Dorr says, there is less time for other academically stimulating activities.

There are problems about comparing people who do not have television, or do not watch much television, with people who do. People who do not have, or use, television may have all kinds of beliefs and child-rearing practices which make it impossible to find an exactly comparable group in the rest of the population. But there was a time when it was easier to make valid comparisons between children in homes with and without television – when television was first becoming popular in this country. During the 1950s, it was still possible to find comparable groups of children in television-owning and non-television-owning homes. Professor Hilde Himmelweit of the London School of Economics carried out a study on television and its effect on children's lives, published in 1958 in *Television and the Child*, which is still of interest today. This study found that the major 'displacement' impact of television was on other entertainment media – children spent less time listening to the radio and going to the cinema. The study also found a temporary decline in book-reading among the TV children, compared to the non-TV children, when TV was first introduced, but after a period of adjustment, book-reading in the TV group returned to the same level as in the control group. There was also a decline in comic reading. The authors pointed out that:

> The reduction was most marked among older children and those of medium intelligence; the bright children were little affected and the dull children read very little in any case.

These are the usual interactions with other characteristics in children and their families, which are not always taken into account by blanket condemnations about the 'effects' of television on 'children'. At the end of the study, the amount of reading among 'dull' children increased and the authors suggest that television may have 'stimulated interest in reading through its serial dramatisation of books'. They also suggest that TV enabled children to become interested in 'a wider range of books than before, including non-fiction'.

Obviously leisure patterns for everybody have changed as a result of the arrival of television, but, as might have been expected, the other leisure industries have adapted and changed too, which have led to new patterns in the current generation of children's behaviour. For instance, a 1986 IBA Research Report, *Children and their Media*, which surveyed nearly 500 four- to 14-year-olds found that 68 per cent of children had a cassette player or radio with earphones, and 65 per cent had their own radio, although radio listening is now primarily for music. Children's tastes for the comedy and drama they once enjoyed on radio are now met by TV. Naturally, the kind of critic who can only accept a medium as 'culture' once it has been superseded in popularity by a new medium, is going to lament children's preference of TV over radio. And inevitably, the focus of disapproval is the feature of the new medium lacked by the old one – in this case television's preponderance of images. Joyce Nelson, in her article mentioned above, categorically states that children 'are so used to watching TV images that they have no capacity for formulating their own images at all', and that, where televised literature is concerned, 'there is no need (or chance) to imagine one's own version of the characters or their environment – it's already been done'.

The unfounded statement that children have no capacity for forming their own images, thanks to TV, is to some extent refuted by work like that of Laurene Krasny Brown, reported in Chapter 5. It is refuted to a further extent by some of the artwork stimulated by programmes like *Hartbeat* descibed in more detail in Chapter 10, and examples like the very vivid recall prompted in the children talking about *Watch* in Chapter 8. More research needs to be done on how children's mental images are affected by television, especially as mental imagery is, in any case, a notoriously difficult entity to prove, or disprove. Many people appear not to have it at all and to be quite incapable of forming pictures in the mind. Cognitive psychologists have been disputing the reality of imagery for years and nobody is in any position to say categorically that mental imagery no longer exists, in children or in anyone else; there are some psychologists who state that it has never existed at all (see Pylyshyn, 1973).

Joyce Nelson suggests it may be 'impossible to conjure any face other than Clark Gable's as Rhett Butler in *Gone with the Wind*'. Conversely, though, it is impossible for some of us to accept Robert Redford as Jay Gatsby, or Laurence Olivier as Mr Darcy, because they simply do not conform to what we think the characters should look like. The power of mental images can thus spoil enjoyment of a competent 'film of a book', rather than the other way round. Mental imagery works both ways, and children's own images of fairytale or storybook characters may be very resistant to the TV versions of them. If the TV images are the first that the children have formed of certain characters, these TV images will become reconstructed in memory over time, just as all images are, and each child's reconstruction is likely to be different. The interpretation of images, as argued in Chapter 8, is something that cannot be taken at face value in any case; the full understanding of how a shot, or series of shots, is selected and arranged, and why, needs to be learned. A televised image, like a photograph or a painting, is never simply a straight copy of its subject: it has always been through a process of selection, arrangement and composition by the artist, photographer or director. People who see TV images merely as pictorial copies of reality are missing the opportunity to educate children about how images and their messages are constructed. There seems no valid reason why TV images should spoil children's ability to form their own. Further, as Laurene Brown's work has shown, TV images can be used to help children create new and more original ones of their own.

TV and cinema-going

Where cinema is concerned, children now use this medium more than adults do. (Included among the current generation of adults are, of course, those children who lost the habit of cinema-going during the 1950s, as reported by Professor Himmelweit. This is a reminder of the importance of taking a historical perspective when talking about 'effects' of media on children. What applies to one generation will almost certainly not apply in every respect to the next one, which grows up with different technology and economic circumstances.) Research carried out between 1985 and 1987 by the Carrick James Market Research company, which continuously monitors children's leisure tastes and habits, including TV watching, found that a much higher proportion of seven- to 19-year-olds 'ever go' to the cinema than do people in older age groups. In 1985, 15- to 20-year-olds were the 'most frequent' cinemagoers. Certainly, many more films are now made for this audience than used to be the case. Thus, despite (and perhaps helped by) the proliferation of television programmes, cinemagoing is now enjoying a resurgence among the young.

The IBA study mentioned above *(Children and their Media)* found that most children had access to a wide variety of media: 94 per cent had a shelf of books at home; 93 per cent had a cassette player; 83 per cent had paintboxes and paints; 83 per cent had a record player; 52 per cent had a computer at home. All had at least one television at home; 43 per cent had a TV 'of their own'. This study also looked at the relationships between TV viewing and use of other media. Overall, watching television did not significantly affect the way children used their other media – either positively or negatively. However, heavier viewers were more likely to read more newspapers and magazines (an encouraging finding for those concerned about TV's effects on reading). Certain types of programmes had a relationship with other media use: heavier drama viewers were more likely to use home computers for writing (as distinct from games playing). Heavier entertainment viewers were less likely to listen to music on the radio. Again, these bald figures suggest that the presence of television in their lives certainly has not stopped children from having access to other media, nor from enjoying and using these other media discriminatingly.

TV and time

How do children manage to fit in all these media with the rest of their lives? And where on earth do they find seven (or more likely, two or three) clear hours a day to watch television? Aimée Dorr, in her book *Television and Children*, has described how children in fact make room for TV in their lives and still manage to do other things as well. She examined the evidence from 'displacement' studies like Himmelweit's and suggests that the process is 'a picture of controlled complex adaptation, not one of radical change or simple substitution'. She points out that, when television was first introduced:

> Children made small adjustments in other daily activities. They slept about a quarter of an hour less each night. They spent ten or fifteen minutes less on homework each day. They decreased

by about half an hour each week the time spent in unstructured outdoor play with peers. They did not decrease their involvement in formal organisations, household chores, extra-curricular school activities or school. And they actually increased their time spent with other family members, again by not more than about a quarter of an hour each day.

Dorr points out that it is only possible to account for the blanket figures of three or five hours average daily viewing so often quoted, by 'many small trade-offs in activities'. She also points out that many activities are shared with television-watching; it is not a question of either/or – either interaction with peers, or watching television. Children (and indeed adults) successfully manage to do both at the same time. Thus, television viewing does not completely wipe out whole hours of other activities; life's various departments are adjusted, trimmed, added to and combined in order to accommodate the various things that children have, or want, to do, including TV watching. And of course, children do not do all their viewing consecutively. As described in Chapter 3, there are peak times when a lot of children watch (in Britain, primarily the one and a half hours of children's weekday programmes) and other times when hardly any children watch.

'TV is great'

Underlying much of the concern about displacement is a view that almost any other activity is better than watching television. Even where the message is reassuring, as in Professor Himmelweit's finding that book-reading was stimulated by TV watching, the underlying assumption seems still to be that it's fine for book-reading to be stimulated by television, but not the other way round. Television is fine so long as it is not 'displacing' other media; hardly anyone appears to take the view that television is fine anyway. No-one dares to say that it might actually be better to watch television than to read, or play. Children's preferences for watching television are thus somewhat brushed aside, even by sympathetic adults. At best, TV watching is to be tolerated, never encouraged or praised. In a 1983 study by Patricia Palmer in Sydney, Australia, reported to the 1986 International Television Studies Conference, Palmer and her colleagues decided to get away from this approach and to start with children's own tastes and ideas:

> It was decided that children's own definitions of the experience of television viewing should shape the direction and concerns of the research project.

Children asked to describe why they liked particular shows often used the words 'fun' and 'excitement' (note: not 'quality' or 'educational'). In the drawings they did, the same feelings of fun and excitement were expressed visually. Children 'consistently drew themselves smiling as they watched TV', says Palmer. They were also fond of drawing dramatic moments or family scenes on TV with everybody smiling. As Palmer points out (almost uniquely among academic researchers), 'the association of fun and excitement with television viewing is not often canvassed in adult discussion or in research'. For adults, the entertainment value – the play value – of television appears to be recognised hardly at all.

Children are aware of this problem in adult perception, too. In Palmer's study, 59 per cent of children agreed with the opinion that 'TV is great'. Only 14 per cent said that this was their mother's opinion, and 12 per cent said it was their teacher's opinion. The child's view of television as 'a nice medium', with smiling faces contrasts with the often-expressed adult view that children only learn 'nasty' and violent things from TV – and that nastiness and violence is what they like. At the time of writing, the Australian soap opera *Neighbours*, is the most popular adult programme with children in Britain. I have asked a number of children, including my own, what, in this extremely bland and unexciting series, is the attraction. Every time, the answers have been variants on: 'People are nice to each other', 'Things work out right, problems get solved', 'It's not like *EastEnders* where people are always having rows'. From this admittedly small and unrepresentative sample, it would seem that some children really do like programmes which show television's 'niceness'.

Palmer's study describes an intense, almost passionate, involvement of children with television – but it is far from unselective and uncritical. This fervour is reserved for favourite shows, and is not given to everything (contradicting the Marie Winn view, described in Chapter 4, that television is a drug, ingested unselectively). Out of the 486 children interviewed, all except nine gave specific programme titles in answer to the question 'What do you watch?' They rarely mentioned generic titles, such as serials or soap operas (although cartoons and movies were sometimes mentioned). They did not talk about programmes they disliked, or did not watch. Palmer and her colleagues also observed children in their homes and noted the same intense loyalty to favourite programmes in children's viewing behaviour. Children wanted to be close to the set, and comfortably settled, in the same position, on beanbags, cushions, blankets or sofas, when special programmes like *MASH* were on. Siblings would squabble and negotiate with each other for optimum viewing positions. Palmer argues that this intensity, and apparent obliviousness to others, is not an example of anti-social behaviour, as some TV critics would infer:

> On the contrary, the deliberate organisation by children of the little space that is left to them shows a keen sensitivity to their social and physical surroundings. Children were adept at manipulating their own environment to achieve their purpose of close involvement with the human drama on the screen.

However, Palmer's subjects did not only relate to the 'human drama on the screen'. Their viewing was the occasion of all sorts of interactions with other people as well. She listed a number of 'forms of interaction', including 'comment, discussion, self-talk, monitoring' and what she calls 're-make'. Re-make is using television as a way of acting out TV and real-life events in forms borrowed from TV, while playing with friends. Palmer quotes eight-year-old Suzi and her friend, playing in Suzi's bedroom. The two girls took turns to speak into a cassette recorder and played it back. They pretended to read the news on TV: 'Today Tasmania was destroyed, but Russia is going to be chopped up to make lots of little Tasmanias.' Palmer describes this as 'social' play in the sense that 'children have control over what they will choose, how they will perform and the kinds of comments they make in the process'. It is also highly co-operative.

A more spectacular example of this kind of skilful re-make of TV techniques by children has recently occurred in Britain. A young teenage boy, Ewan Phillips, had a habit, similar to Suzi's, of turning his whole life into a news bulletin. This became the basis of a very funny children's programme, produced by Central Television, *News at Twelve*. In the programme, Ewan plays a boy called Kevin Doyle, who gives a weekly news roundup of his family's exploits, for example, the ongoing struggle over 'control of the TV station':

> Back home, there has been intense hand-to-hand combat in the living room today, as rival factions struggle for control of the TV station . . . The living room has been divided for many years, with, on one side, the pro-*EastEnders* faction led by Mrs Doris Doyle, and on the other, the hardline sports fanatics, led by Mr Doyle. A fragile truce was arranged by Sharon, who managed to keep the peace for a few days by hiding the *TV* and *Radio Times*. But fighting broke out again today, as *Dallas* clashed head-on with indoor bowls from Nantwich.

It would be impossible for an audience of children to appreciate this kind of parody (backed up by authentic location filming of the Doyles' home and neighbourhood, and interviews with interested parties) without intimate knowledge of the style of news bulletins. The joke – applying newsgatherers' inflated language to the mundane activities of an ordinary family – is a sophisticated one, because it is primarily linguistic, rather than visual. Nevertheless, the programme was very popular and I was surprised to find that my eight-year-old was just as capable as her teenage siblings of seeing the funny side of items like the account of Sharon Doyle's wedding in terms of the Andrew/Fergie romance ('The cameras began to gather at No. 3 when it was learned that Mrs Doyle had cancelled her planned trip to Tesco's . . .'). In fact it was the eight-year-old who insisted I come and watch *News at Twelve* as she was sure I'd find it useful for my book. *News at Twelve* is an excellent example of children's television itself teaching children to be sensitive to, and critical about, television and its characteristic clichés.

The fact that children sometimes use television series and characters as the basis of their fantasy play is often criticised by teachers, as showing a failure of imagination. It is surely anything but. Imaginative play, as I have argued earlier, can only really be play if it is something chosen by children themselves, and reflects their current preoccupations and concerns, not those chosen for them. If the argument between Shane, Jane and Mike in *Neighbours* arouses children's anxieties in its portrayal (albeit banal) of the problems of loyalty and betrayal between friends, then it is only natural that 'playing Shane, Jane and Mike' will turn up in imaginative play. Equally, a fascination with words and the peculiar things that can be done with them can give rise to elaborate play 'scripts', as in the case of eight-year-old Suzi, and 14-year-old Ewan, who were stimulated by news techniques to comment on their own lives and on their views of the grown-up world. This kind of observation, parodying and 're-making' is almost certainly going on in every playground and family in the country. Adults could learn much about children from it, if only they had the humility to listen.

10 | Children's responses to television

Every year, the special department of the BBC which handles solicited correspondence receives millions of items of mail. The majority of this is from children. In the last year of *Superstore* (now replaced by *Going Live*), it was calculated that over five million letters were accounted for by this programme alone. Many of these were simply competition entries. But hundreds of thousands of letters are received each year with more detailed responses to programmes. They include entries for creative competitions (over 54,000 for *Blue Peter*'s 1987 competition to design a cover for *Radio Times*); requests (10,000 children write in for *Hartbeat* Fact Sheets each year); paintings, drawings, collages, designs and even animated films (53,000 sent to *Hartbeat* in its 1987 series); general knowledge questions, jokes and ideas for inventions (*Corners*); ideas for things to do (*Why Don't You?*) and birthday wishes (*Andy Crane*). Some of this correspondence is used in programmes. Much of it is acknowledged, (*Blue Peter*, for instance, answers every one of its annual 100,000 letters), but not all of it can be. And this is just the correspondence which is solicited.

Unsolicited correspondence is also sent in response to favourite programmes and characters and this may be dealt with either by the individual programme makers, or by the BBC's special Programme Correspondence Unit. According to Roy Thompson, Deputy Head of the Children's Department, children's unsolicited letters are overwhelmingly favourable – they write when they are pleased about something, not when they are angry, as adults do. Even though they may not get a response, the readiness with which millions of children write in to TV programmes suggests that children treat television as a medium with which they feel they can have an amicable dialogue.

This is in line with the findings of Patricia Palmer, quoted in the last chapter, which showed that children saw television as a 'nice' medium, associated with smiling faces, 'fun' and 'excitement'. Children appear to treat television as a friendly presence in their lives. Even when their letters or paintings have very little chance of being seen on screen, they continue to respond to popular programmes actively and enthusiastically. This dialogue with the medium is not based on a belief that fictional characters are 'real' (from about age seven onwards, most children know that they are not). It appears to be based on the belief that favourite TV programmes are made by people who are basically well-disposed towards children and will look kindly on friendly overtures from them.

This contrasts strikingly with adult distrust of TV, based on the potent image of a monster enslaving and corrupting the young (see Chapter 4). I decided to confront the 'monster' by visiting the offices of two programmes who are particularly close to their audiences – much of what goes into the programmes depends on audience response – to look at the kinds of contributions children send in. I also talked to the programme makers about how these contributions are handled and how they see the child audience. The first programme was *Hartbeat* which features a 'gallery' of children's artwork in every programme. The second was *Corners*, which is based entirely on questions sent in by children.

art with a small 'a'

'What we're trying to do,' says Chris Tandy, producer of *Hartbeat*, 'is to take the capital A out of Art. It's not just an elite subject, done in studios – it's everything and everywhere. We want to open children's minds to all aspects – pleasing design, materials, new arrangements of objects.'

Hartbeat (which used to be *Take Hart*, which, in turn, grew out of *Vision On*), has been opening children's minds to the artistic possibilities of cardboard, coal, tinfoil, water, twigs, corks, newspaper, buttons, fingerprints, (to name a few of the many items used in the programme – not just as media, but also as implements), for the last 13 years in some form or other. In all its manifestations it has been presided over by the energetically versatile Tony Hart, who describes himself as 'a jack of all arts' who 'just dropped into TV by accident, found it exciting, and wanted to share what I'd found'.

In all the hundreds of thousands of pieces of artwork submitted to his programme over the years, Tony Hart has found that some things don't change in children's art – and some things have changed, particularly, he thinks, as a result of television:

> Children see a great deal more from TV. This is good if TV interests them, then they can be persuaded to go and find the real thing.

Tony himself seems to have little trouble persuading children to go and find the things that he and his assistants demonstrate in the programme. If, one week, the studio artists make collages with tree bark or leaves, the following week, they are inundated with pictures using this technique. Sometimes, though, children themselves come up with an original medium – and this is one quality the programme-makers and presenters look for in the work sent in. As Tony pointed out:

> Sometimes a child has found a medium we never thought about working with. It's nice when someone picks up an old electric plug and thinks: 'That looks like a cat's face'.

When I visited the *Hartbeat* office, two examples of such originality had just come in: one a design made entirely out

153

of paper ring reinforcers, sent in by a 12-year-old from Lancashire, with neat step-by-step instructions attached for how to use the technique. A five-year-old had sent in a picture using a marbling technique based on very watery water colours. Originality and honesty are what Tony and his team look for – honesty is a quality he fears children begin to lose after about the age of seven. They then have a tendency to become rather imitative and anxious to please and conform; Tony sees it as part of the programme's brief to get children away from this conformity and to experiment with different materials and methods:

> We want them to think first, what they want to work *in* and then what they want to work *at*. Children's art can get a bit predictable after age seven. We probably get more pencil drawings copied from comics than anything. But sometimes, if a copy is really good, we'll use it.

Other perennially favourite topics with children, through the years, are clowns and owls. Tony thinks there are good reasons for this:

> A clown is a sort of disguise; they are fun and happy and have painted laughs on them. They can be very brightly and vividly coloured and it doesn't matter, because clowns are meant to look like that. Owls look like specs, teacher, profs., authority. Children are much, much happier with discipline around them.

The other thing that children like – and Tony has found this from extensive travels round the country meeting children in schools and playgroups – is 'getting mucky'. He has to be careful in the programme not to use materials that are going to require a lot of cleaning up by someone else. Parents can become indignant about this. Nevertheless, he believes in the value of messy materials when properly controlled – particularly for the very young (but not food materials, to which his viewers object quite strongly): 'If you take printing ink and roll it out on formica or plastic, very little children, even one-year-olds, can start off by making extremely delicate handprints.' For a recent series of *Hart-*

beat, Tony was filmed demonstrating these techniques at one nursery school, 'where there was a community of delightful people with damp cloths at the ready'. He explained what happened:

> We put a sheet of paper over the ink and got children to make marks with nails and pencils. We pulled off the paper and there was a mirror image of their marks on it. They were fascinated – they went on and on and didn't want to stop. One three-year-old wrote her name. When the paper was taken off, the other children couldn't see anything odd at first. But the one who had written her name noticed that it was a mirror image, the wrong way round. You could see her mind working – that was much better than if I'd haughtily explained in words about mirror images.

Future series of *Hartbeat* will be using more film sequences of Tony working with children in schools to demonstrate such moments of insight. Tony is constantly trying to extend children's artistic ambitions in this way. From his years of experience of looking at children's pictures, he knows what their limitations are, and this gives him ideas for widening their horizons:

> For instance, children don't mix media very much. I mix marker pens and chalk together. You can show a young child how to create depth in a picture – distance or overlapping objects. If you use coloured markers and white chalk, you can use the chalk to fade down bits of your picture, fade a black mountain into shadow for instance.

The other great virtue of the *Hartbeat* approach to art is demonstrated in this example – that none of the media or techniques cost very much. Felt-tip markers and chalk, ink, bits of rubbish or natural materials are within the price range of virtually all children. Tony also aims to be flexible:

> With every project I work on, I try to make it something that can be adapted to any age of child. The great advantage of television is that you can entertain such a lot of people at the same time . . . The other great advantages are that you can

show how things are done, the composition, the colour. I can look at a piece of artwork and say, 'Ah, how do you think she's doing that?' The camera can be used to demonstrate collage, assemblage, rubbings, prints.

For Chris Tandy, Tony's producer, this ability to demonstrate such a wide range of techniques is the great asset of *Hartbeat*'s televisual approach to art, which he does not think would be possible in any other medium. And it doesn't necessarily matter if it doesn't inspire children to go and do the same thing themselves. Chris Tandy believes that just watching is valuable too:

> There is great pleasure to be got out of three minutes watching someone creating something on TV. You don't have to imitate. You go and look at paintings just for the pleasure they give you – you don't go round the National Gallery or the British Museum necessarily wanting to do the same thing yourself. You enjoy it as a pleasing experience.

It is a pleasing experience that millions of children continue to opt for. One of *Hartbeat*'s proudest boasts is that it persistently attracts higher audiences than cartoons scheduled against it on ITV.

'Putting my brain in gear'

Nine-year-old Richard from Leeds spent hours of his time designing a 'Car of the Future' to send in to *Corners*, BBC's general knowledge programme for five- to seven-year-olds, for their Inventions spot. His car featured a camera, radar, 'driving arm', 'killer wheel', 'elastic knife' and 'electric arrow' – all carefully signposted on his brilliantly coloured design. Although some of the car's features suggest that Richard, like many nine-year-old boys, sees the future as being somewhat bloodthirsty, the accompanying letter suggested that, given a choice, he himself would rather spend his time peacefully at the drawing board:

Dear Corners, Here is my entry/car of the future. I've just put on what's come into my head. I did a few but this is the best one. It's a complecated picture. I don't think I could draw it again. I took a lot of time and patience on this picture and I had to put my brain in gear.

Putting their brains in gear is an obvious characteristic of the children who sent in ideas for inventions to *Corners*. Where the inventions were small and ingenious, the children sent the inventions themselves. For example, ten-year-old Graham sent in a 'two-way bubble blower' – a clothes peg with two bubble blowers attached to it. Six-year-old Laura had sent a re-useable envelope, using staples to re-fasten a used envelope. The inventions came in two broad categories – first, the totally fantastic, which showed ingenuity and imagination in devising, for example, extraordinary machines for automatically turning on the TV:

At 3.50pm on Friday an alarm cracks the glass which moves a ball down a tube; it lands on a see-saw, flings brick in the air, hits see-saw, makes finger slide off and fall on button.

Also in this group were 'a playground bully-catcher' from a six-year-old Merseysider; a 'bow-tie of leisure' – featuring water and milk carriers, a calculator, a sick bag, and a radio, all attached to the bow-tie, from an Essex eight-year-old; and a 'get-your-brother-to-shut-up machine' from ten-year-old Fiona.

The other group of inventions were genuinely practical ideas which could be put into use, if an enterprising manufacturer took them on. They included skis to fit over a baby buggy for travelling over the snow, from a Kent nine-year-old; a wonderfully simple way for adult or older child and baby to have a bath together, from an eight-year-old Essex girl – a 'double bath' with a small bath attached to the side of the big bath; a 'bird-table organiser' for putting bird food out during snowy weather when you don't want to go outside (a spade to put out of the window to push the snow aside, with a bowl of bird seed attached to the topside of the blade, which tips out when the spade turns over). There was also a self-threading needle, based on the principle of the plastic fasteners used on sliced loaf bags. As many of these ideas as possible were made up and demonstrated in the programme.

Producer Anne Gobey was not entirely surprised by the range and ingenuity of the inventions. She was already well aware of the diversity of children's thinking from the kinds of questions they sent in to be answered on the programme. When I spoke to her, one had just arrived saying: 'Please Corners, is there a God? And if there is, where does he live? And how is the world made?' They hadn't quite worked out how to answer that one, but hoped to find a way. A great many of the questions derive from an intense curiosity about how things work – which makes for some lively demonstrations in the studio, such as presenter Simon Davies making candyfloss in a specially borrowed candyfloss machine. Anne is always struck by the 'quality of fun in the letters – like little cartoons'. Again, the Palmer finding that children see TV as a source of fun, amusement and friendliness is echoed here.

Television as persuader

Most adults would accept that the influence of programmes such as *Hartbeat* and *Corners* is beneficial; these programmes come under the acceptable headings of 'quality' and 'educational' – even though their producers are most anxious to avoid being seen as worthy, and stress the entertaining aspect so valued by their young contributors. However, these programmes also demonstrate the success of TV programmes in persuading children to do things. This success can be interpreted in a sinister light: the monster rears its ugly head in many guises. For instance, one of the most popular arguments in favour of the view that television persuades people (particularly the young) to behave badly and violently is based on the fact that programmes like

Hartbeat or *Blue Peter* do influence children's behaviour – in a positive way. Surely, therefore, the 'bad behaviour' in *Grange Hill*, or in *The A Team*, must be equally influential in a negative way.

The clinching point of this type of argument, which is frequently mentioned (it came up with great conviction in a *Kilroy* discussion programme about children and TV that I took part in, in April 1988), is that advertisers spend millions of pounds buying time on television to persuade people to buy their products, which must mean that television has a powerful influence all round. (Whether advertisers are right in their supposed belief that TV successfully persuades people to buy things is another question and will be dealt with in Chapter 12.) This argument, in its crudest form, goes: If television can successfully persuade people to go out and buy shares in British Telecom or a packet of Kellogg's cornflakes, television must be equally successful in persuading people to go out and rob banks, shoot criminals, blow up buildings and drive cars through a busy city at 150 miles an hour. *Hartbeat* persuades children to collect household rubbish and make pictures with it. Therefore, *Grange Hill* must be equally successful in persuading children to go out and bully other children, run minor protection rackets and drop their aitches.

It should not be too difficult to spot the fallacy in this argument. If you are somebody who needs to buy breakfast food for your family, or has a bit of spare capital to invest, you will be able to see the difference between somebody persuading you to buy cornflakes (which you need to do anyway) or to buy shares (which is in your own interests) and somebody persuading you to kill, maim and destroy, which is almost certainly something that you don't particularly want to do. Such behaviour would cause great distress to other people, it would probably land you in jail and it may well be against your religious principles. Thus, in the one case, the advertisement is suggesting to you a course of action that you are quite happy to follow anyway, whereas in the other case *The A Team* is suggesting (if, indeed, it is suggesting – depicting and persuading are not synonymous) a course of action which you are unlikely to follow in your wildest dreams. If you are a child who is at a loose end and *Hartbeat* gives you some bright ideas for using up your old sticker collection, you may well be influenced to do what the programme suggests. But if you see bullying and protection rackets on *Grange Hill* (particularly when you see the culprits being punished or ostracised) you may not be so keen to follow their example, because bullying other children is not such a pleasurable activity as having a good time with your mates at some activity or other.

This is not to idealise children, or to deny the attractiveness of anti-social behaviour. While children do have a strong desire to be law-abiding, helpful, and creative, as evidenced by the millions of positive responses they make to programmes like *Blue Peter*, *Hartbeat*, *Corners* and *The Really Wild Show*, the attraction of creating mayhem is also a powerful one. Programme makers need to be sensitive to this attraction and be on their guard against exploiting it, as most producers of children's programmes are. Nevertheless both they, and the children who write to them, recognise that a programme with no mischief-makers in it would be difficult to make either entertaining or convincing, since conflict is the essence of drama and no child is good all the time.

The following point may seem so obvious that it is hardly worth saying. Nevertheless, in the light of the bad press that television's influence on children consistently receives, it needs to be said again that the childhood attraction to mischief, and even downright brutality, is not a recent development. It has always been there and appears to be intrinsic to certain periods of childhood and to certain types of child. Not portraying it in stories or on television will thus not do away with it. Developmental studies have shown that there seem to be peak ages for aggression, at around two to three years old, and later in the early teens. Other periods of childhood are relatively calm. There are obvious and long-standing sex differences in aggression too; boys, on the whole, are more likely to be aggressive than girls, and men are much more likely to be violent than women. Both sexes watch television – indeed, women watch more – so television cannot be held to account for this gender difference in anti-social behaviour. As long as television is almost exclusively blamed for violence in society, the real origins of these differences can conveniently be left unexplored.

Children also take time to develop a sense of morality – concepts of fairness, justice, equality and appreciation of other people's points of view may not be apparent until around the age of five or six, and will take longer to be put fully into practice. Much development of a moral sense depends, obviously, on what is going on around children as they grow up. It may be harder (though not impossible) for children to be peaceful if their parents are violent, or generous if everybody they know is mean. Television is unlikely to be able to override the influence of family and community. Its influence will be strongest when it is going in a direction in which the child (or adult) viewer already wants to go. This is what advertisers rely on; this is what will make a programme or commercial influential.

Appropriate endings

If a programme shows bad behaviour like bullying in school, the direction in which a child audience will want to go will be towards the defeat of the bully. Children have a strong sense of fair play and a need for just and appropriate endings to stories, or storylines. For instance, here is a group of 12-year-olds discussing the way Den Watts exploits and betrays his wife Angie, in *EastEnders*, as described in David Buckingham's book about the series, *Public Secrets: EastEnders and its Audience*:

> *Natasha* Angie's too soft though. She always says, 'I'm sorry Den'.
> *John* If he was doing that, you wouldn't go out with him. He goes out with Jan, right, and you wouldn't stick up with it. I would either leave him, or . . .
> *Fiona* I wouldn't give him a second chance.
> *Natasha* She should smack him in the face or boot him one.
> *Lee* I know what my mum would do. She'd get a frying pan and knock him over the head with it.
> *Fiona* And if I was Angie, I would have got Jan and booted her one.

The sympathies of these children, although expressed in terms that probably wouldn't please Mary Whitehouse and her supporters, are with the victim, who, they feel, should give the bully (or, in this case, Den, the heartless husband) his come-uppance. Their sympathies do not go to the bully. Many adult critics seem to find it difficult to make this important distinction between showing a bad action, and approving or disapproving of it. Yet Grant Noble's work on children's liking for television characters, described more fully in Chapter 6, shows that part of children's enjoyment of 'villainy' comes from 'negative identification' – the desire to disapprove of bad behaviour, not to imitate it. Enjoying J.R. doesn't mean approving of J.R. – quite the reverse. And, although Den is undoubtedly a popular character in *EastEnders* (*Rodney* 'That's what I like about him. He's a bit of a bastard.'), the children interviewed by Buckingham show no signs of either approving his behaviour, or wanting to emulate it.

Come-uppances need not always be in the form of the violence proposed by Natasha and Lee above, although such violent suggestions, again, do not necessarily mean that children see the solution to every conflict as a wallop with a frying pan. The research of Bob Hodge and David Tripp, mentioned in earlier chapters, indicates that children can well understand the symbolic nature of violent endings – the defeat of evil by good, as represented in a shoot-out, a fight, an explosion, or a villain's destruction. (For those who are unconvinced by this point, an eloquent defence of the symbolic value and meaning of traditionally violent fairy tales and myths can be found in Bruno Bettelheim's book *The Uses of Enchantment*.) Nevertheless, in a realistic modern setting, violence may not be an appropriate way to bring about the right and just denouement. A Children's Film Foundation film transmitted in May 1988, called *Terry on the Fence*, took the daring step of trying to make dramatically explicit how some children become bullies. The 'villain' of the story, Leslie, a teenage punk, turns out to have been neglected and brutally treated by his obsessionally houseproud mother. The 'hero'/victim of the story, Terry, defeats the power of the bully by showing loyalty to and pity for him, not by destroying him.

There was plenty of physical aggression and some bad language in this film, which aroused a great deal of criticism (88 phone calls of complaint, but only from adults, were logged after it was shown.) Such incidents, particularly bad language, are extremely rare on children's television. Roy Thompson, Deputy Head of the BBC Children's Department, points out that including bad language in a children's programme is completely counter-productive in terms of impact. It arouses so much complaint that it detracts from the main point of the story. Sue Elliott, who handles complaints about children's programmes for the IBA, has a similar opinion.

Such incidents will always offend people who see the morality of a story entirely in external details, rather than primarily in the motivations of the characters. But the ability to explain morality in terms of intention, rather than solely in terms of action, is a sign of moral maturity and there is evidence that it can be better facilitated in children by film than by other media, as the American research done in 1973 already referred to in Chapter 5 found out. Few children in the age group for which *Terry on the Fence* was intended (eight- to 13-year-olds) would be likely to interpret the message of the film as in favour of bullying or bad language. Children who watched it with me, aged eight, nine, 13 and 16, accepted the bad language as part of the story's realism (and, initially, as pivotal to the plot, since the hero runs away from home after being told off for using a swear word). What my child audience found hard to accept was the lack of adult sympathy for the boy hero, in particular on the part of a rather insensitive and obtuse head teacher. This character, and not the teenage bully, aroused the strongest protests in these children.

Television elicits direct responses from children which, on the whole, are favourable and trusting, creative and positive. Children rarely complain or criticise in their spontaneous responses to the medium, and when they are asked for specific contributions, like artwork or competition entries, they give them in impressive numbers and with great imaginative diversity. Although the children who write, or send contributions, in response to programmes are a self-selected sample and thus cannot be assumed to be typical of the whole population, the extent to which their response is positive is impressive – particularly when contrasted with the mainly negative responses of adults (also a self-selected sample.) But there are other ways which indicate how children respond to television – ways in which they take programmes and commercials and their messages and put them to use in other areas of their lives. Television does influence the activities of children – but not always in ways which we would expect or predict. The next chapter will look at some of these ways.

11 | Television spin-offs

As discussed in the last chapter, television gives children many ideas for activities directly related to programmes and which are actively solicited by programme makers. But, of course, children may be given ideas for activities in more indirect ways. Television can affect how they play, read, use their leisure and buy things. The culturally pessimistic response would be to assume automatically that children will be influenced for the bad, rather than for the good, in all these activities. Television stops them reading (John Naughton, *The Observer*, May 1988). Television creates a taste for violent toys (*Campaign*, September 1987). Television destroys childhood (*Kilroy*, BBC, April 1988). And so on.

These views receive considerable cultural respectability from broadcasting's primary competitor, the press, which seldom publishes articles in praise of television's influence on children. The then newly appointed Director of the Broadcasting Standards Council, Lord Rees-Mogg, was given generous column space in *The Independent* in May 1988 to state his negative views and fears about the effects of television on the young. He wrote that he intended to follow the 17th century philosopher, John Locke, and the 19th century political theorist, John Stuart Mill, in defining the state of childhood as one which is 'imperfect' and in which children have no right to 'individual sovereignty', by virtue of not having 'the maturity of their faculties'.

According to Mill, and Mogg, children require 'instruction and training' for the mind. Few would quarrel with this, especially those who, unlike Lord Rees-Mogg, are actively engaged in the rearing, teaching, nursing and entertaining of the young. Many would agree with Mill and Mogg that not to provide such training is a 'moral crime'. Where some of us would find cause for concern in the arguments for the Broadcasting Standards Council is that they proceed primarily from negative rather than positive concerns. One point of concern is, firstly, in how 'instruction and training' are defined; it could be argued that leisure and freedom are as important as formal schooling and discipline in the healthy growth of the mind, and television has a part to play in both leisure and freedom. Secondly, there is cause for concern in the implication that television and more formal 'instruction and training' are somehow antithetical. A realisation that some of the training and instruction which children need is already being provided in a positive sense by British television (in the classroom, for example, as described in Chapter 8), makes no appearance in Lord Rees-Mogg's argument. The idea that the Broadcasting Standards Council might act more in children's interests if it defended what broadcasters are trying to do for children at the moment, seems similarly foreign. The idea that children themselves should have some say in the debate is completely unheard of.

The concept of evidence – that is, of systematically studying what and how children themselves learn, or do not learn, from television – is a key missing element of Lord Rees-Mogg's concerns. When the evidence is examined, the ways in which children incorporate television into their lives are both more complex and less sinister than Lord Rees-Mogg and those who agree with him might think. An instructive example is the example of reading.

Television and books

A common concern about the side-effects of television is that it stops children reading. A study carried out by Susan

Neuman in the United States in 1984 took measurements of time spent watching television in over two million children – aged nine, 13 and 17 – in eight different states, and compared these measurements of viewing hours with measurements of reading skills in school, and with children's use and enjoyment of reading as a leisure activity. These comparisons were subjected to a number of computer analyses, taking into account sex, ethnic background and socio-economic status, and no overall relationship was found between reading skills, leisure reading and television watching. In other words, for the sample as a whole, the amount of television watching did not relate to being a good or a bad reader (as measured by comprehension, vocabulary and study skills in school) nor did it relate to how much children did, or did not, read in their leisure time. If television stopped children from reading for pleasure, or from learning to read, we would expect that, the more television they watched, the poorer would be their reading performance, and the less they would read for pleasure. This study found no such relationships.

There were some interesting variations within the sample. For instance, the results revealed that children who watched a moderate amount of TV (between two and three hours a day) had higher reading achievement scores than children who watched less (although this was less likely to be so in California and Rhode Island, for some unknown reason). When it came to time spent reading for pleasure, again, no relationship was found between longer hours spent watching television and fewer hours spent reading. In one group – nine-year-olds – there was actually a positive relationship: that is, the more they watched television, the more they read.

A more recent study, involving 13,000 11- to 16-year-olds in Britain in which researchers at Exeter University focused on one evening's activities, found a similar unexpected relationship between heavy viewing (five or more hours) and increased amounts of reading (two or more hours spent reading for pleasure). Among less heavy viewers and readers there was no relationship at all to suggest that the more children watched, the less they read. With both boys and girls, book reading declined in the older age groups (perhaps reflecting an increasing amount of homework), and television viewing also declined among girls, but not among boys. The authors stress that the relationship between different leisure-time activities is a complex one which varies for different reasons. Their study only asked about the previous evening. Viewing habits obviously vary over time and it may be that other patterns would be forthcoming on different nights of the week, or at other times of the year. Nevertheless, such a large sample provides fairly convincing evidence of the lack of support for the 'displacement' theory of television's effects on reading.

Susan Neuman argues that children are motivated to read, or to watch television, not because of the time available (or not available) but because of enjoyment: 'When students defined reading as an enjoyable activity, they tended to do more reading during their free time.' Neuman points out that:

> Children enjoy television and often do not enjoy reading. Instead of blaming television for this phenomenon, it makes sense to try and change this attitude . . . We must develop ways to extend their understanding of its [reading's] compelling uses outside the school setting.

Books and the box

A variety of ways of persuading children of the 'compelling uses' of reading was explored at a conference called 'Books and the Box' held in London in February 1988 by the Children's Book Circle, at which TV producers, writers, performers, market researchers and representatives of the book and toy trade, met to consider 'the relationship between children, books and television.' Children's author

Helen Cresswell, who has written a number of series for television, including *Polly Flint* (ITV Central) and *Moondial* (BBC), argued that writing for television had made her a better writer:

> *Polly Flint* was the first decent novel I ever wrote. I didn't know the meaning of the word 'plot' until I wrote *Polly Flint*. Writing a serial for television meant that there had to be at least five points in the story when something had to happen to make people turn on next week.

Helen Cresswell described this process as 'television doing the book world a favour'. She pointed out that the process of writing both the TV scripts and the book of *Polly Flint* side by side was 'a new art form'. She has 'always been delighted with the TV versions of my books. Something is added rather than subtracted. Actors can give characters a depth and strength not in the book. The production of *Moondial* gave it a depth and strength not in the book.'

Both *Moondial* and *Polly Flint* have been successful paperbacks. Televising a dramatised version of an existing book can hugely increase its sales in the shops. When Eric Hill's *Spot* books were televised, their publisher, Heinemann, found that sales of the books doubled from 10,000 to 20,000 in a year. The sales of *Thomas the Tank Engine* books doubled from 20,000 to 40,000 when the series was shown on ITV.

Paul Stone, a drama producer for the BBC, who also spoke at the conference, pointed out that the television/publishing relationship can work both ways. He had commissioned distinguished children's writers such as Leon Garfield and Bernard Ashley to write original drama serials especially for children's BBC – *December Rose* and *Running Scared* respectively. They were very different kinds of story. *December Rose* was a historical adventure about a cockney chimney sweep who became involved in political corruption, set against a background of life on a river barge. *Running Scared* was a contemporary story, set in the East

End of London, about an English girl and her Asian friend becoming involved in a protection racket, with the theme of racial prejudice and misunderstanding running through it. Book versions of both became best-sellers.

Having a book dramatised on television is a guaranteed way to increase its sales. It will also dramatically increase the number of borrowings from libraries. Angela Beeching, executive producer of the BBC's *Jackanory* (the storytelling programme) has been asked by librarians throughout the country to give them advance warning of what books will be featured in the series, so that they can make sure these books are in stock. Evidence like this suggests that television, far from preventing children from reading, can act as a powerful stimulus to reading. Television has also revived the art and power of direct storytelling – *Jackanory* being a long-running example. At the conference, actor and storyteller Tony Robinson described how he had developed his own technique of semi-improvised television storytelling, as in his dramatic rendering of *The Odyssey* for children's television. He had seen the excitement of direct narrative when rehearsing for a National Theatre production of *The Oresteia* and the actors had had to tell some of the text in their own words, and behind masks: 'The masks appeared to change at key dramatic moments in the text.' For Robinson, story telling is about 'excitement and passion', of which the immediacy of direct improvisation to the camera, rather than reading from an autocue, is a part. Again, the book version sold well. One child I know, who was only eight years old, loved it so much that he asked the librarian for a copy of Homer's original.

The key to explaining this ability of television to stimulate children into reading book versions of TV stories may well be the enjoyment factor, mentioned by Susan Neuman. Watching a series on television clearly does not put children off wanting to go through the story again. On the contrary, they repeat the enjoyable experience by reading the book. This desire to follow up a story, of which they already know the outcome, in book form, further suggests that children are well able to perceive the distinctions between the pleasures of television viewing and those of reading: they are different kinds of enjoyment and one is not a substitute for the other. One avid 15-year-old reader explained: 'When I've enjoyed something on television, or as a film, I can't wait to read the book, just to find out more about all the characters.' She cited *Gone with the Wind* as an example: 'I enjoyed the book more than the film, because there was so much more detail and depth in it.' Thus, the pleasures of reading and viewing are not mutually exclusive. Rather, they appear to be complementary to each other. If this is generally so, it helps to explain the findings (mentioned above) that children who watch a lot of television also read a lot. The evidence described here suggests that television does not displace reading. It provides a different form of satisfaction which can both complement and help to promote reading.

There are still, as there always have been, large numbers of children who do not, and will not, read for pleasure no matter how great the encouragement of parents and teachers. One such group has traditionally been boys of all ages, but particularly adolescent boys. In 1987, the Book Trust mounted a television campaign aimed at older teenagers called 'Let's throw the book at you', in which advertisements on London Weekend Television, using popular youth presenter Jonathan Ross as front-man, promoted the idea of reading as 'a generic activity'. No particular book, or publisher, was featured but viewers were invited to phone in for a free book and a 'Top 40' list of books. Four and a half thousand phone calls were received in response to the first promotion on 30th October, and a further three thousand came in after repeats of the 'commercial' in the next two days. Ten per cent of the first group of calls (460) came from under-16s, and of these, the majority were boys. Sixty five per cent of those wanting humorous books were boys; 60 per cent of requests for

171

music books were from boys and 80 per cent of requests for science fiction came from boys. Lindsay Pearson, projects manager of the Book Trust, who spoke at the Books and the Box conference, was surprised at this breakdown, in view of boys' traditional resistance to reading as a pastime. She felt that this form of televised promotion was an excellent way of getting boys to show an interest in books.

TV toys

One of the greatest areas of anxiety to do with children and television concerns toys. In 1986-7, the BBC's decision to purchase the American cartoon *Thundercats* caused a flurry of debate, with children's television, usually ignored by media commentators, suddenly receiving unprecedented coverage. Articles were written in *The Listener*, *The Independent*, *The Guardian* and trade magazines, such as the advertisers' journal *Campaign*; a Channel 4 *Right to Reply* special devoted itself to the issue; there was a seminar on the subject at the 1987 Edinburgh Television Festival. The reason for all this concern was *Thundercats*' direct connection with a range of toys made by Mattel. The series was based on these toys, rather than the other way round (that is, with toys being developed after the series, which has happened in this country with all popular series from Muffin the Mule in the 1950s, down to Postman Pat today). Mattel helped to finance the costs of making the programme, which has led to such programmes being described as 'programme-length commercials'. This direct commercial link between toy manufacturers and programme makers is common in America, where there are around 50 toy-based commercials on the air at any given time, but it is new to Britain. The purchase of *Thundercats* aroused alarm at the prospect of what Brian Rotman, writing in *The Listener* (9 October 1986), called 'the most gullible consumers the market can locate – young children' being subjected to 'feature-length commercials persuading viewers to buy the characters'.

While there is cause for concern at the independence of children's programme makers being compromised by the invasion of toy manufacturers into their creative decisions, the real questions at issue as far as the welfare of children is concerned, have been somewhat obscured in this debate. The real questions are to do with what children like to play with and how; and what television's role should be in drawing their attention to appropriate playthings. The question of 'What is an appropriate plaything?' arises here, as does the question of who decides on its appropriateness: child or adult or advertiser? The simple fact that children do need toys, and that adults do need bright ideas for birthday or Christmas presents, and therefore somebody has to meet those needs somehow, has been in danger of becoming overlooked. As one toy manufacturer (whose company makes He-Man and She-Ra toys) wrote, in answer to a critical article by Michael Leapman in *The Independent*, in August 1987:

> Mr Leapman has an evident concern that parents will come under pressure to buy these toys. If the toys are well made, safe, entertaining and good value for money . . . why is this a bad thing? Unless, of course, Mr Leapman has evidence to suggest that these toys are being bought under duress, *in addition* to the expenditure parents would normally plan on for their children's toys . . . (I assume, of course Mr Leapman does expect parents to have to buy some toys at some time).

The 'gullible' audience

The concern about the effects of toy advertising on children arises from the belief, as expressed by Brian Rotman, that young children are 'gullible' and can therefore be persuaded into wanting something that really is not suitable or enjoyable for them. As I mentioned in an earlier chapter, where playthings are concerned children can be very resistant to adult persuasion that certain kinds of playthings are better for them than others. Every parent knows about the toddler who plays with the packaging in which her present was wrapped and ignores the toy, and the child who treasures the plastic pony bought at the jumble sale, rather than the expensive doll bought by Grandma. My eight-year-old daughter and her friend Nicky have a current game called 'Funny Offices'. They use use chunks of decorated polystyrene packaging with pencils sticking out of them, as portable phones, and they wear high-heeled shoes cast off by Nicky's mum, to look the part of Dallas-type secretaries (and they also employ a strange sub-Texan accent). During this absorbing game there is not an expensive nor an educational toy in sight. The girls do not lack toys; they live in families with a total of seven children between them, and in which there are, therefore, more than fair shares of accumulated Little Ponies, Barbie dolls, Sindy dolls, board games, Lego, toy cars, jigsaws, model railways, plastic tea sets, chemistry sets, skates, skipping ropes, bikes, books, comics, records, tapes, felt-tip pens and craft equipment – to name only what I could see last time I looked.

We may not like this enormous accumulation of consumer goods acquired by our children – but it is we who buy these things, not they. Maybe we parents should not feel too apologetic about this. In my experience, most of these toys do give good, if sometimes intense and short-lived, play value, often for more than one child, and are thus worth the money. As an adult, a Barbie doll would not be my choice – but when I was seven, I would have given my eye teeth for one, had it existed at the time. My tastes have become more sophisticated since then, just as I now prefer bitter chocolate to bubble gum, but I don't expect my own eight-year-old to share them yet. So the objection to toy-led programming cannot be against toys per se, nor, I would argue, is it fair to object to the type of toys shown in these programmes just because we, as adults, find them unappealing. Although we may object to excessive commercial influences, and to shoddy goods, we still need to accept that, in our society, it is normal for children to have toys and that these toys are different from the toys we played with.

Even the poorest children will usually have some people around them who will want to buy them the occasional birthday or Christmas present. Seventy-one per cent of seven- to 17-year-olds have pocket money too – an average of £1.32 a week, according to a recent survey of this age group by the Carrick James Market Research company. This is supplemented by occasional gifts from parents or relatives, by extra money for specific purposes (like comics or outings) and payment for odd jobs. Although the spending power of children as a whole market is thus worth millions of pounds, individual children have relatively small amounts to spend on items like toys. They rely on grown-ups to buy most of their toys for them. So is it parents who are gullible?

According to Elisabeth Sweeney, psychologist and Research Director of the Children's Research Unit, an agency which carries out market research into children's attitudes to advertising and consumer products, parents nowadays are more ready to listen to their children when it comes to making spending decisions. This is as much a matter of prudence as of indulgence:

> Where the toy market has diversified so widely, we find that parents are less confident in their selections of toys for their children and take serious note of the things they have been asked to buy . . . While they may feel little sympathy with some ranges, parents acknowledge that it is money wasted to try to instil their own choices on their children. Many claim that the most disappointing purchases have frequently been the surprise gift – the item the child didn't ask for.

In other words, when parents are not guided by their children's advice, they often end up wasting their money.

175

Children are undoubtedly influenced by television programmes in their choice of toys. Thundercats, He-Man, She-Ra, Care Bears, Postman Pat are all cases where there are links between merchandise and programmes – that is, the characters featured in the programme can also be bought as toys, or as product labels. Even programmes which TV's severest critics would count as worthy, such as *Play School* and *Rainbow*, have merchandising spin-offs. Indeed, for many independent children's programme makers, particularly those who make cartoons, which are labour-intensive and thus expensive, a failure to attract merchandising link-ups may mean that there is no money for more than one short series – this happened to a delightful British cartoon series called *Willo the Wisp* which came and went in the early 1980s.

We may feel that there should be no link-up between programmes and toys and other products – but this is to deny the fascination with programme characters that children can have, and that will lead them to want to become more involved with these characters. Just as the teenage *Gone with the Wind* viewer could not wait to read the book, to find out more about Scarlett O'Hara and Rhett Butler, so younger children will want to extend their enjoyment of Postman Pat, or the Care Bears, into their own play experience. It is very natural for them to want to make these characters their own and to integrate them into their fantasy lives, as long as the fascination with the characters lasts. This may not be very long; one popular series will be superseded by another, and children grow up. Such transience is not peculiar to children's tastes in toys; it is true of many of life's experiences.

The desire to bring characters out of the screen, into everyday fantasy games and everyday life, would not be seen as an unhealthy reaction in the case of the reader wanting to buy the book of *Polly Flint* – but there does seem to be more disapproval in the case of toys. Perhaps this arises from the puritanical tradition of disapproving of objects that are only for playing, rather than for improving the mind, which, many people seem to believe, books invariably do, simply by being printed. The intellectual value of play experiences involving hands, eyes, bodies, objects (i.e. toys) and co-operation with friends may be less appreciated. As Elisabeth Sweeney pointed out, toys are a way of belonging to the all-important peer group, during the primary school years: 'No child wants to be the only one playing with a toy rejected by his or her peers – although being the first with a craze enhances their status considerably.' Most children over eight, she added, are sceptical about advertisements: they believe that 'at least 50 per cent of adverts don't tell the truth'. If a toy advertisement is inaccurate or misleading, children will be disappointed at the point of sale and this is not to the manufacturer's advantage. In the case of collectable toys 'inaccuracies (in advertising) will decrease the chance of repeat purchases'. So, whatever we adults may think of them, toys like Little Ponies and Thundercats, which are extensively collected, do not appear to disappoint children.

In fact, when children's tastes in toys are looked at more closely, TV-linked toys are far from being the most popular. The Carrick James Market Research company carries out an annual survey on several hundred seven- to 12-year-olds around the country each year. In 1987, the most popular toys with boys were Lego (16 per cent mentioned it among their 'toys most liked at the moment'), Transformers (15 per cent), bicycle (15 per cent) and computer games (14 per cent). With girls, tastes were spread more widely. Most popular toys were: dolls (11 per cent – mainly accounted for by seven- to 10-year-olds); Monopoly (13 per cent – this was also liked by 11 per cent of boys and is one of the few examples where girls' and boys' enthusiasms coincide); 8 per cent of girls mentioned My Little Pony; 9 per cent mentioned Barbie. Eight per cent of girls also chose bicycles – in the younger age group, i.e. seven- to eight-year-olds, almost as many girls (11 per cent) as boys (13 per cent) were fond of their bikes. The differences between the sexes become much more marked as adolescence approaches, but are more fluid among younger children, with the exception of the doll/Lego split. Toys linked to programmes were not among the most popular – only one per cent of children mentioned Thundercats, although the programme would have been transmitted at the time, and none of these were girls. Other TV-linked characters, such as He-Man and She-Ra also did not figure highly. The highest percentages of responses were for 'other' unnamed branded games (20 per cent), reflecting the fragmentation of the toy market. These figures represent individual mentions of many different playthings, not numerous enough to provide a group score. Thus children's tastes in favourite playthings do not seem to be particularly strongly influenced by TV-linked toys.

The most urgent concern arising from the link between toys and television is the possible effect that an increase in toy-led programming could have on children's programmes generally. Will the invasion of toy-based programmes push out more original, more expensive material, as has happened in the United States? If so, then we have genuine cause for concern, especially when broadcasting becomes deregulated and the insatiable demand for material for new satellite and cable channels means that programmes financed by toy-makers become one of the cheapest and easiest ways of filling air time. In the United States, the effective pressure group, Action for Children's Television (ACT), headed by Peggy Charren, a concerned parent, has been pressing for more choice for children and for the labelling of toy-based programmes for what they are: 'The programme you are watching is based on Toy X and is designed to promote the sale of that toy by Company Y.' ACT does not want toy-led programming banned. They want to see a wider range of programming for children and, as mentioned, clear identification of 'programme-length commercials'. A British version of ACT, British Action for Children's Television (BACTV), is hoping to pursue the same principles in the

UK, as well as to defend the best of the mix provided by children's television at the moment. This mix, including the presence of *Thundercats*, was defended by Anna Home, Head of the Children's Department at the BBC, at the Edinburgh Television Festival in 1987: 'Kids enjoy it [*Thundercats*] hugely – and why shouldn't children have the right to relax to television sometimes, as adults do? . . . If it's followed by John Craven's *Newsround*, we find more children watch that as well.'

TV as cult

Television is now part of children's culture in a way it never was for many of their parents. My family did not acquire a TV set until I was 12. My own children have grown up with television from birth. To me it was a novelty and a luxury. To them, it's just part of the furniture and the daily routine. Television will become part of my children's childhood memories, just as clustering round the radio on Monday at 7.30 pm to listen to *Journey into Space* is part of mine. I hope that the older ones will remember our great Wednesday evenings in Spring 1988, when we used to watch *MASH* at 9pm, followed by the gripping, horribly truthful and brilliantly funny *A Very Peculiar Practice*. This told of the tribulations of a university medical practice succumbing to Thatcherite pressures and entrepreneurial asset-stripping by a glamorous, especially imported American Vice-Chancellor. We would all watch it on video the next day, so we could savour the full wit and literacy of the script and the discomfitures of Bob Buzzard once more. I hope they will fondly remember the crisps we consumed, and the coffee, and the intense discussions about who the Machiavellian Vice-Chancellor reminded us of. I know I will.

Children's programmes have begun to be an object of nostalgia: one of the bestselling videos of 1988 was a tape of early editions of *Watch with Mother*. Writing in *The*

Listener in December 1987, Andy Medhurst attempted to extract a moral from the current wave of revivals for early children's programmes: 'It is difficult to see recent plans to reshow creaky, patronising and woefully outmoded programmes like *Andy Pandy* as anything other than a reactionary pining for the nursery.' However, what comes across from his own memories, enjoyably recounted in the article, is not 'reactionary pining' but a vivid sense of how much his favourite TV programmes contributed to the way his own childhood was organised. He fondly recalls when he 'enjoyed *Thunderbirds* the first time round, developed a strong affection for Clarence the cross-eyed lion, and was introduced to the special joys of the deliberately corny joke through the good offices of Basil Brush.' The programmes that seem to be most affectionately remembered by people writing later are not necessarily the outstanding ones; they are the bread and butter series which marked out the daily routines of their childhood lives. Medhurst opens his article by challenging his readers to complete the slogan: 'It's Friday, it's five to five and it's . . .' (The answer to this, of course, is *Crackerjack*.)

Young children's programmes, with their regularity and their frequent repeats, lend themselves particularly to this kind of nostalgia. Among current teenagers, *Clangers*, broadcast in the early 1970s, has a special significance and there is a rock group called The Soup Dragons (after the denizens of The Soup Mines on the Clangers' home planet, you will remember). A record enormously popular with my teenage children and their friends was *The Trumpton Riots* by a now disbanded group from Liverpool, Half Man Half Biscuit, whose lyrics on unemployment 'in the Chigley end of town' seemed all the more powerful for the apparent innocence of their setting, drawn from memories of childhood television programmes. The lyrics of their songs illustrate Andy Medhurst's point that young children's programmes do have hidden ideological 'agendas' – a point I also made in an article for *The Listener* called 'Feudalism for the Under-Fives' in January 1977. These lyrics show that, as young people grow up, these agendas do not remain hidden. Children develop the sense to see them for themselves.

In a *New Musical Express* special supplement in April 1988, young rock stars and actors recalled their favourite children's programmes, and how these were associated with significant childhood experiences. Programmes mentioned included *Stingray* ('because of Aqua Marina, the mute sea-girl. I loved her.' – Holly Johnson); *Tales from Europe*, especially *The Singing Ringing Tree*, also *Robinson Crusoe*, *Barnaby Bear* and *The Munsters* (Ali Campbell of UB40); *Pinky and Perky* (The Rhythm Sisters – 'We had all the plates, bowls and LPs which we used to dance to. Debi was Perky and Mandy was Pinky.'); *Double Deckers* and *White Horses* (Janice Long). Some interviewees mentioned enjoying adult programmes as children: presenter Gary Crowley loved *The Virginian* – 'Me, my brother and sister all played the different characters. My brother was the Virginian and I was Trampas.'

The NME supplement, though extremely well-researched, relies heavily on jokiness and spoof. (Fans of *Rainbow* – with its singing trio and Zippy, the puppet with a zipper for a mouth – will recognise the following: 'We should look instead into the sick heart of *Rainbow* . . . The sick cult of Rod, Jane and Freddy followers, The Rainbow Warriors, can be recognised by their love of kicking bears, their fear of zips and the fact that that they are all buskers on the London Underground.') There are many people who would disapprove of this way of treating children's television, as a corruption of innocence. Anyone else, who is actually interested in young people's tastes in TV and how these connect with other views, should read it. No serious student of the subject should be without its list of One Million Most Essential TV Programmes Ever Made – from *The Addams Family*, through Michael Bentine's *Potty Time* to *The Woodentops* and *Z Cars*.

Taking TV over

One of the songs sung by the supporters of the not-very-successful Fourth Division football team of which my sons are faithful devotees, goes:

> We know someone you don't know, Yogi, Yogi,
> We know someone you don't know, Yogi, Yogi Bear.

The last verse begins: 'Yogi's got an enemy, Stockport, Stockport' (or whichever the opposing team happens to be). This is sung, with complete good humour (virtually no crowd violence – virtually no crowds – in the Fourth Division) to the tune of *Camptown Races* – an excellent example of the spontaneous blending of two oral traditions. To the teenagers and young adults who have grown up with television, *Yogi Bear* and *Rainbow* are as much part of their lives and memories as their parents' and grandparents' fond reminiscences of apple-scrumping and Knock Down Ginger. Television programmes don't stay 'in the box'. Characters, stories, images and ideas enter into the lives of their young viewers and are taken over by them, so that they become something quite different from what the original programme-makers intended. Through these kinds of spin-offs, children 'colonise' television and make it their own.

12 | Children and television advertising

In an article called 'Researching children's markets' in the market research magazine *Perspectives*, in April 1987, the authors described children and their spending power as 'a time bomb'. This lurid description was prompted by the realisation that British children aged five to 16 have around £6 million per year in pocket money. The authors further pointed out that, since 43 per cent of households now have two or more TV sets, the prospects for those wishing to advertise to children looked inviting. Children are seen, according to this philosophy, as a highly desirable market, which any enterprising manufacturer should be ashamed not to exploit: 'Children's brands will be forced to compete in a far more aggressive marketplace than ever before', concluded the authors enthusiastically.

Such sentiments are enough to confirm the worst fears of those who see television as basically destructive of childhood and its innocence. The child as consumer is a particularly unattractive phenomenon, conjuring up images of a greedy, spoilt brat, forever demanding more of what he or she has seen in television commercials – sweets, toys, clothes, equipment and money – from harassed parents, who are forced to succumb to this human 'time bomb'. The imagery of marketing 'aggression' reinforces those critics of television, like Marie Winn, who see its hold over children as wicked and irresistible. The idea of advertiser as aggressor is paralleled by a softer, but equally corrupting image of advertising: what one researcher, Brian Young, has called the 'child-as-innocent and advertiser-as-seducer' syndrome.

There is no way in which this book would support a philosophy of aggressive, or indeed, seductive, marketing to children, in order to relieve them of their couple of pounds a week pocket money. Advertisers need no defence in any case; they are prosperous enough to be more than capable of defending themselves. However, from the perspective of a concern for children, there are a number of questions that need to be considered before we accept uncritically the view of television advertising as either violent rapist, or as soft seducer of the innocent. In the first place, what needs to be asked is whether all advertising aimed at children (or indeed at adults) is really aggressive, in the sense that it has a forceful and destructive impact on its target. Equally, what needs to be queried is how seductive advertising is, in the sense of insidiously persuading impressionable minds to do things, or want things, they would otherwise not have done, or wanted.

We need to look more closely at the concept of gullibility in children. To what extent are children (and distinctions between age groups have to be made here) 'taken in' by advertising – and if they are, to what extent does this influence their purchasing behaviour, or that of their parents? There is also the extent to which children are not 'taken in' by advertising: they know that commercials are trying to sell them something and they may, or may not, be prepared to go along with the message of the commercial, depending on whether it is advertising something that they want, or not. Is this good or bad? A further important question has to be: to what extent are parents influenced by their children in their purchasing decisions? Are they at the mercy of greedy, demanding consumer toddlers, or do they have more control over the situation than either the marketers or the TV critics believe?

Commercial v. public service broadcasting

Much of the research on children and advertising which could help to answer these questions (as on children and television generally) has been done in the USA. Since the US broadcasting system is primarily a commercial system, with massive commercial sponsorship of programmes and constant interruption of programmes for advertisements to be shown, information about children's responses is obviously both commercially useful, and of concern to those working with or for the welfare of children. Children in the UK have grown up with a very different broadcasting system, in which public service, rather than commercialism, has been the shaping force, thanks to the fact that the pioneering role in the development of broadcasting was taken by a public institution, the BBC. This public service role was taken as a model by the more recently developed commercial Independent Television system. The duty to inform and educate, as well as to entertain, is stressed in the Independent Broadcasting Authority's guidelines for programme makers.

Commercialism as a shaping force is thus much less widespread in UK broadcasting than in the US, and whether coincidentally or not, independent (as distinct from market) research on children and advertising in the UK is also sparse compared to the US. However, things may change when the full effects of deregulation of broadcasting are felt and there is a greater choice of commercial channels in this country. At the moment, as the figures quoted in Chapter 2 indicate, the majority of programmes most enjoyed by children (and nearly all *children's* programmes most watched by them) are BBC programmes, which have no advertising. Children in this country are thus continually made aware that it is possible to have television channels which are not in the business of persuading them or their parents to buy things; they are aware of, and use extensively, a television service whose aims are solely to inform and entertain, not to sell.

Advertising messages

Possibly as a result of this, advertising styles in Britain appear to be rather different from those of the US, relying much less on the hard sell, and much more on wit, humour and clever dramatic and filmic techniques; in other words, they are more like mini-programmes. In his *Financial Times* TV column in May 1988, Christopher Dunkley queried whether, enjoyable as they are, British adverts, like the one for British Telecom with Maureen Lipman as a Jewish granny, or the one for K shoes, in which a woman wearing non-squeaky shoes catches her two-timing lover out and tips a bowl of pasta over him, actually succeeded in selling the product:

> They strive, even compete, to entertain the viewer and to a remarkable extent, they succeed . . . In the US, as far as I can establish, the first question asked about a commercial is: 'How much product will it shift off the shelf?' . . . An awful lot of British commercials are better designed to win Brass Bunnies than to increase through-put on the supermarket shelf.

These clever and entertaining qualities in British commercials are certainly picked up by children. The entertainment value of a commercial, rather than its informativeness or persuasiveness, is what seems to appeal to them most. For instance, a survey of 400 six- to 14-year-olds published in January 1988 in a report by the market research company, The Research Business, discovered that by far the commonest reason given for liking an advertisement by all age groups was that it was 'funny'. When asked what their favourite types of commercials were, the majority again named 'funny advertisements'. Next came advertisements with cartoons, followed by ones with animals (although the popularity of cartoons was obviously greater with younger than with older children). After humour, the quality in commercials most valued by children was the music – particularly so in nine- to ten-year-olds and 13- to 14-year-olds.

'Liking the product' came only sixth in a list of nine qualities mentioned by children and at the bottom of the list came 'informativeness'. Interestingly, 'liking the product' was mentioned more often (15 per cent of replies) by six- to eight-year-olds than by any of the other three age groups

(6, 10 and 4 per cent respectively). More will be said below about age differences in responses to commercials – but this finding bears out the general truth that younger children are much less likely than older ones to make a distinction between the message and the product: if they like the product (for instance, a toy) they will be more likely to say they like the advert, even if it is not a particularly lively advert. Older children are able to distinguish between the excellent qualities of humour and dramatisation in the Carling Black Label advertisement, and the not necessarily excellent qualities of the beer itself. Like adults, they can enjoy the ad without automatically, if at all, liking or wanting the beer.

This is an important point to remember when noting the ads that children most like, which include a large number for adult products. In the Research Business survey, toy ads attracted the highest votes from six- to eight-year-olds, and also in nine to tens and 11 to 12s, but in smaller proportions. With 13 to 14s, those for beer came top. All groups mentioned Anchor butter (the one with the dancing cows) and beer ads. Ads for crisps and Andrex toilet paper were also generally popular. Older children liked Mates condoms and Oxo ads; younger ones went for Transformers; 11 to 12s liked the ones for Weetabix and Pepsi.

In the 1988 survey carried out by the Children's Research Unit mentioned in the last chapter, the top three advertisements were Anchor butter, British Telecom (featuring Maureen Lipman) and Carling Black Label (featuring a surfboarder surfing into a pub and asking for a pint of aftershave). In all these adverts, many of them for exclusively adult products, both surveys found that humour, an amusing story and clever effects were what appealed to children, with the product being incidental.

Persuasion and action

It is very flattering for an advertising agency, and presumably for its client, to learn that its commercial is popular, amusing and a winner of a Brass Bunny, as Christopher Dunkley puts it. The fact that 'informativeness' and 'liking the product' come so low on the list of even older children's priorities in judging adverts, seems not to be a cause of concern to advertisers. Yet information – telling people about the product in order to try to sell *that* product (as distinct from other products) – is what advertising is supposed to be about. Whether, as far as children are concerned, the popularity of an advert actually translates into 'through-put on the supermarket shelf' seems to be a question that is only addressed in the vaguest terms by market research. Yet this is a question of crucial importance in addressing the issue of whether or not children are bludgeoned or 'seduced' by commercials into wanting and buying things that they would not have otherwise wanted.

To take the example of Anchor butter – a commercial popular with all age groups in both the surveys mentioned above. It's an extraordinary case since butter does not even have the vaguely glamorous appeal of the forbidden, as in beer and condom adverts. Yet children love this commercial. The authors of the Research Business report speculate that the purchase of Anchor butter:

> May well be vulnerable to children's influence on Mum. Children often accompany Mum to the supermarket and are, on occasions actually sent to pick up various items as they journey round the shop. It is in this situation that Anchor might be benefiting from advertising . . .

The words 'may well be' and 'might be' betray the fact that these researchers do not know whether this is how children behave or not. In my own all-too-extensive experience of supermarket shopping for a large family over nearly two decades, I have never brought the children with me if I can possibly help it, and I do not often see parents who do (toddlers and babies perched uncomfortably in special seats are a different matter). Boys over the age of five are a very rare sight, girls slightly less rare. I do not believe that children enjoying Anchor's dancing cows on television have the slightest effect on 'Mum's' shopping behaviour – but of course I may be wrong. The point is that we do not really know, since there is not much follow-up research into children's and families' actual buying behaviour, although a great deal of market research is done into their attitudes and opinons. The processes involved in translating a persuasive message into behaviour are notoriously difficult to trace, as many social psychologists have discovered. Just because people find a message convincing, does not mean they will act on it. For example, in a national survey of mothers of new babies (published under the title *Infant Feeding* in 1980), researchers working for the Department of Health and Social Security found that the majority of mothers who chose to bottle feed their babies, still thought that breast-feeding was better for the baby. The case of anti-smoking propaganda is another good example. People are convinced by it, but continue to smoke.

Remembering commercials

Deciding to go out and buy a product seen advertised on TV depends on many things – not only on how people *feel* about commercials, but also on what they remember of the information in them. No matter how imaginative a commercial is, it is unlikely to 'shift products' if, the next time the family goes shopping, nobody can remember the product's name, or what it looks like.

To find out the relationship of advertising techniques and recall of information in advertisements, we have to turn to academic research. A study of 500 children, ranging from pre-school to juniors, carried out in America in the mid-1970s, tested children for their verbal recall of the brand names in a series of commercials. This study found that the greater the children's visual attentiveness to the screen – attracted by characteristic commercial qualities like fast

189

action, visual changes and music – the less likely they were to remember the name of the product. In other words, increased visual attractiveness resulting in closer attention, seemed to have an adverse effect on children's ability to remember what the advertisement was for. In another American study in 1972, two versions of a commercial – one with a special offer, the other without – were shown to children of first, third and sixth grades (aged six, eight and eleven). The sixth graders remembered most – but, among these older children, those who saw the special offer version remembered the product symbol less well than the children who'd seen the commercial straight, with no extra persuasive message.

Media research in cognitive psychology, such as my own research on editing, mentioned in Chapter 5, suggests that messages are better remembered when they are simple, clear, not divided up by too much cutting, and have good co-ordination between pictures and words. This is even more important for children, who have greater cognitive limitations the younger they are. Thus, although advertisements may seem worryingly 'aggressive' or 'seductive' to us, the ability of entertaining commercials to translate persuasiveness into buying behaviour may actually be limited, rather than enhanced, by clever production techniques. This is speculative and it is not possible to say for sure that Maureen Lipman in the British Telecom ad has not persuaded children, when they grow up, to forgive British Telecom its many shortcomings. (It would be interesting to know how many children actually realise what the BT ad is for . . .) But the point is that, just because children like and enjoy adverts, there is no really strong evidence that this attractiveness automatically translates into children wanting or buying things they wouldn't otherwise have wanted. There is even, as we have seen, some evidence to suggest that the reverse might be the case, if we accept that people can't buy a product unless they can remember what it is.

What is a commercial?

A crucial question about the ability of advertisements to confuse or mislead the young is: how soon, and how, do children recognise the difference between commercials and programmes? The possibility of confusing advertisements with programmes is increased when personalities who appear in comedy, drama or even documentary, also appear in advertisements. The IBA Code of Advertising Standards and Practice explicitly forbids the use of cartoon characters or puppets featured in either BBC or ITV children's programmes in commercials. In the United States 'host selling' (using a character from a programme in an advert) is forbidden in commercials embedded in, or directly adjacent to the relevant programme. Before this ruling, some American research published in 1975 on the use of 'Pebbles', the little girl from *The Flintstones* cartoon, to advertise cereal, found that younger children (three- to seven-year-olds) were much more likely to express desire for the cereal when the commercial was shown in a tape of *The Flintstones* than when it was shown in a tape of a Bugs Bunny cartoon. The adjacency of the programme seemed to favourably affect young children's perception of the commercial. Young children were also more likely to say (wrongly) that Pebbles had been eating cereal in the programme. Such confusions did not occur with older children.

There are a number of American studies, such as those contained in *The Effects of Television Advertising on Children* published in 1980, which have shown that the ability to distinguish a commercial from a programme improves with age. Younger children (four- to eight-year-olds) were much more likely to say that a commercial was 'more funny' or that it was 'short', compared to a programme. Over-eights were better able to recognise the commercial purpose of commercials. In Britain, the Children's Research Unit noted similar differences between children under and over eight years old. Five-year-olds

191

could talk about advertising from their own point of view as 'showing you things to buy' – whereas eight-year-olds and older children were able to perceive that commercials had a specific purpose: 'They're trying to sell you things.' These older children were able to see the *advertiser's* point of view. Studies using non-verbal material – asking children to sort out, or point to, different pictures and to decide whether they come from commercials or programmes – have found the ability to distinguish commercials from programmes in children as young as two. However, the key ability – to recognise the 'persuasive intent' of advertising – takes much longer to develop and is probably acquired at around the age of eight.

Brian Young, the British researcher mentioned above, has argued that the ability to distinguish persuasive intent is related to the development of linguistic ability – in particular 'metalinguistic' skills, or the ability to 'stand back from language and make a judgement on the language itself'. Such judgements include the ability to understand puns and double meanings; an appreciation of metaphor and simile and an awareness of ambiguity in language. Such abilities are all required in the comprehension of the persuasive intent of advertising – and of the various techniques that advertising uses. Although Young is referring primarily to verbal language, the ability to 'read' television's visual techniques is also implied here. It may be that visual literacy of this kind develops earlier, or later, than verbal literacy, or the two may be related. At the moment we have very little knowledge about this interesting question. In order to be 'advertising literate', it is obviously essential for children not only to be able to understand verbal ambiguities, but also to appreciate the kinds of *visual* jokes and references that advertising uses. One example of such references is the series of lager ads featuring Griff Rhys Jones intercut with scenes from classic black and white movies – war films, Westerns, and comedies such as *Some Like It Hot*. It is only possible fully to see the joke in these commercials by appreciating the various film genres being gently parodied in them. Whether or not viewers are persuaded to buy more lager by being able to spot and enjoy the visual double-entendres is a much more open question, and raises once again the not necessarily direct relationship between persuasiveness and actual behaviour.

In an interesting corroboration of Young's thesis, that full advertising literacy involves metalinguistic skills usually acquired at around the age of eight, the research carried out by the Children's Research Unit, mentioned earlier, found just this kind of difference between children under and over eight. Children over eight were much more likely than under-eights to say that '50 per cent or more of adverts don't tell the truth'. In fact, advertising is bound by the IBA code to be 'legal, decent, honest and truthful'. What the children seem to be acknowledging here is the ability of advertising to stretch the literal truth, or to suggest ambiguities – the kinds of metalinguistic qualities described by Young. Elisabeth Sweeney, employed by the Children's Research Unit and author of their report, argues that, where products aimed at children, such as toys, are concerned, it is very important that commercials do tell the truth:

> Children don't like to feel they have been conned. They can be subject to major disappointment if the toy doesn't do what they expected – this extends to exact colour references and whether or not batteries will be needed.

Sweeney warned against the use of fantasy in commercials for children under seven, because her research had found that this led to unrealistic expectations of toys. She pointed out that young children found it difficult to integrate visual and auditory information and that, for a toy commercial to be effective, 'it is essential, with the younger child, to give very clear product demonstrations'.

Sweeney's paper quoted above was written for an audience of toy manufacturers and their advertising agencies and it is interesting to note that she stresses the value of informativeness and accuracy in commercials for products aimed at children – values that children themselves rate rather low in their judgements of commercials. This raises the important question of what the point of advertising actually is. Is it to entertain, amuse and perhaps mislead? Or is it to sell products by persuading people that the product is worth buying? Is an acceptable advert from the children's point of view one that persuades them to buy products, or one that simply amuses them? Paradoxically, if Sweeney is right, the more truthful, informative and accurate a toy advert is (that is, the further away from ambiguity and indirect persuasive techniques), the more likely it is that it will persuade children to want to buy the toy. So what do we want from advertising when it comes to children? Adverts which are clever, entertaining, joky, ambiguous and possibly misleading, may actually be less successful in persuading children to want things. Adverts which show recognisable portraits of child-like behaviour, are realistic, give accurate product information and are not misleading, are likely to be more effective in persuading children to buy, and to buy more than once – at least where children's own products are concerned.

The intelligent consumer

At the heart of anxiety about the effects of commercials on children is the concern that children's natural innocence and developmental limitations will make them vulnerable to the seductive, or aggressive, blandishments of advertisers. As the research above suggests, this concern is more appropriately confined to children under eight. By the time they are eight, most children appear to be capable of recognising the persuasive intent of commercials and to believe that adverts are 'not true', in the sense of not being a fully objective account of the product. It is probably fairly safe to say that the attitude of children over eight to commercials is one of enjoyment and appreciation, combined with a degree of scepticism. They are not likely to be easily 'taken in' by persuasive techniques. However, the fact that they are not taken in, does not mean that they will refuse to buy an advertised product – an important point, sometimes overlooked in discussions about children's responses to commercials. If a child likes Weetabix, or wants a particular Lego set for Christmas, a commercial announcing that Weetabix is giving away special stickers, or a Lego ad for a new addition to their spaceship range, may very well be influential in reinforcing the child's wishes, and in telling his parents how these can be fulfilled (for example, where the products are available). The older child may also have a reasonable amount of pocket money, and the necessary ability to calculate and save so that he or she can buy their own toys, snacks or reading material. Commercials, even those perceived to be hyperbolic, may positively guide the child's judgements about this.

In an interesting and seemingly unconscious revelation of their own bias, the academic authors of *The Effects of Television Advertising on Children*, mentioned above, state: 'The economic realities of commercial broadcasting offer clear evidence that commercials can sell products to viewers, *even* [my italics] when their sales intent is understood.' It would be just as logical for these authors to say that commercials can sell products *especially* when their sales intent is understood. It does not seem to have occurred to these writers that intelligent viewers, children included, may be perfectly prepared to be persuaded to buy something, if it seems a reasonable course of action and is going to provide them with something they want. Understanding the sales intent of an advertisement is not just a way of 'seeing through' it to the sinister hidden persuaders on the other side. It can be a useful adjunct to making intelligent consumer choices, which children need to learn to do.

While we all need to be concerned about hyper-aggressive or ultra-seductive sales techniques, and their unwanted invasion of children's lives, there is no need to go to the other extreme and suggest that selling things, or telling people to buy things – or, indeed, buying things – is morally wrong. One cannot help wondering whether academic commentators like these ever have to go shopping. Persuasion is not inevitably a sinister activity; if people could not persuade each other to do things from time to time, civilised relationships would be impossible. Much depends on the degree of equality between the parties involved. Where advertising is concerned, although advertisers have the greater persuasive power, in terms of large budgets, access to the mass media, skilful techniques and so on, the consumer has direct power over the purse strings. Unless the consumer is prepared to go out and spend his or her money, all the persuasive techniques of the advertiser have no force at all – and there is many a failed campaign to testify to this.

Where older children are concerned, the evidence suggests that they are as able to handle the information and techniques of advertising as are adult consumers; they may even be more sceptical about advertising than adults are. School projects, such as the one described in Chapter 8, can also help to make younger, or slower, children more critically aware of the techniques and intentions of advertising.

The role of parents

Where the younger child is concerned, the effects of advertising have to be mediated by parents. Much of the concern about the impressionability of children is rightly to do with the very young. For instance, Brian Rotman writing in *The Listener* in 1986 about toy-based cartoons, described young children as 'the most gullible consumers the market can locate'. He took the 'enormous box office success' of toy-based films such as *The Care Bear Movie* and *My Little Pony* as evidence that accompanying adults are 'scarcely less gullible'. As an adult who has sat through both *The Care Bear Movie* (an excellent movie) and *My Little Pony* (a truly awful one) in the company of a young daughter and friends, which I suspect Mr Rotman has not done, I would suggest that his use of the word 'gullible' here is being stretched to unacceptable levels.

It is not gullible for little children to like Care Bears, attractive and comforting (if somewhat expensive) soft toys; it is perfectly normal. The movies Rotman mentions are some of the very few examples of full-length feature film entertainment which are suitable and accessible to very young children. As such, they are a perfect godsend to adults, in full possession of their faculties, who want to introduce their children to the pleasures of cinema-going, and are looking for enjoyable ways of spending an afternoon at half-term. The difference in quality between *The Care Bear Movie* and *My Little Pony* was an interesting talking point between me and Elinor – she, too, enjoyed the first more than the second and we were able to identify a number of reasons why this was so. We did not feel any desire to add to our collection of Care Bears and My Little Ponies – a collection which has provided some enjoyable hours of play in its time – as a result of seeing the movies.

In assessing the impact of soft-sell commercials on very young children, it needs to be recognised that such young children are not in a position to go out and buy what they have seen for themselves. Children's success as consumers depends on their being able to persuade their parents, and other adults, to go and buy things for them, and there is evidence to suggest that not all parents are stupid enough to be totally dominated by their children. Advertisements may very well mislead and confuse the very young, and we may be right to deplore this. What we can be fairly sure of, to return to the crucial, and always uncertain, connection between attitudes and subsequent behaviour, is that a four-year-old being 'taken in' by a My Little Pony ad does not automatically lead to that four-year-old owning My Little Pony. An adult has to be persuaded to buy the toy. So how 'gullible' are adults? How much do they yield to pressure from children against their own better judgement?

In a survey, published in the report *Advertisements, Children and Christmas Time*, carried out for the IBA in both 1985 and 1986, parents and other adults were asked about their attitudes to toy, beer and snack advertisements at two different stages. They were surveyed first at the end of October, and then at the end of December, just before Christmas. Mallory Wober, the author of the report, predicted that, if the huge seasonal increase in the volume of advertising for toys, drinks and snacks were creating extra pressure for parents, then their attitudes would be different in December (after being subjected to this pressure) to what they were in October. The survey asked people to rate their agreement or disagreement with such statements as: 'Advertisements are an acceptable feature of the current season on TV'; 'Advertisements provide worthwhile information for children and parents'; 'Toy advertisements cause bad feelings when parents and children disagree about what they can afford'. Most of these statements did not produce either strong agreement or disagreement; people seemed fairly neutral about them, though the statement about 'bad feelings' produced a fairly high degree of agreement. Unfortunately, as with so much research on people's attitudes to products and to adverts, this study did not provide evidence about what people actually went out and *bought*. What was interesting, however, was that there was virtually no change in people's attitudes between October and the end of December. Despite having been subjected to almost permanent bombardment of toy, drink and snack adverts in the run-up to Christmas, the respondents in this study seemed fairly impervious to it. If their buying behaviour was linked to their attitudes, then it too would have been unaffected by the advertising bombardment.

Parents do not wish to deny their children every request and 'not giving in to pressure' from children is not necessarily a virtue at all times. A child who *never* succeeds in persuading a parent to stop being busy and take him or her swimming, or to buy Nike trainers rather than Woolworth ones, is a bit of a deprived child, just as the child who *always* succeeds will be horribly spoilt. Elisabeth Sweeney points out that:

> Children soon learn that only a limited number of requests will be met, so they more realistically limit their requests to things they really want . . . Where the toy market has diversified so widely, we find that parents are less confident in their selections of toys for their children and take serious note of things they have been asked to buy . . . While they may feel little sympathy with some ranges, parents acknowledge that it is money wasted to try to instil their own choices in their children.

In a paper given to the same audience of toy manufacturers as Elisabeth Sweeney's, Yvonne Millwood, a Senior Advertising Control Officer for the IBA, described some IBA-sponsored research into parental responses to children's requests for various items, including toys. This study, carried out at Surrey University, found that a large number of family conversations about commercials began with the 'Can I have . . .?' opening ploy. The majority of the parental responses were of the 'I'll see . . .' variety – either negative or non-committal. Many responses were conditional, depending on the price or suitability of the toy, and on whether the request came near the child's birthday or at Christmas. Parents were asked how they felt about having to make negative responses and more than half said they didn't mind; having to refuse their children did not make them 'feel bad'. About a quarter confessed to feeling irritated by the experience. The majority of parents said their children understood and, on the whole, accepted refusal, although 20 per cent said the child sometimes 'got cross' when refused.

This is not exactly a picture of massive family conflict generated by commercials, nor does it provide any evidence that parents are 'gullible'. It suggests that parents are, on the whole, well in control of their children's consumption of leisure products – and that buying items for children is a matter of negotiation, with parents having the final say.

There are two sides to every message, including advertising. All researchers have rightly drawn attention to the importance of children understanding the 'persuasive intent' of advertisements. Adverts are not just objective descriptions of products, or amusing little mini-dramas; their aim is to persuade the viewer to buy the product. However, the corollary of recognising the sub-text of 'persuasive intent' in the sender of the message, is to recognise the potential 'intent not to be persuaded' in the receiver of the message. This is where the linguistic and textual analysis of persuasive techniques – the study of 'illocutionary force', as linguistic philosophers would put it – needs to meet up with psychological knowledge about how information is processed by the people receiving it. The study of psycholinguistics and of semantic memory reveals that messages go through many transformations in the course of being perceived, stored in memory and recalled later. Just because the sender intends a particular meaning, it does not follow that the meaning will be grasped; and if it is grasped, it does not follow that it will be acted upon.

We know a great deal about the content of advertising messages and something about how children perceive and understand this content. But what they actually *do* after receiving the message is a different matter again. What evidence there is suggests that both parents and children tend to do what they want to do – and that advertising may reinforce them in their decisions. One of the great strengths of the human mind (which not even the most powerful computer intelligence has yet managed to match) is its power of refusal. It can learn to understand every nuance of meaning, both explicit and implicit, in a persuasive message;

it can be emotionally moved by the message; it can swear blind that it will obey the message. And, at the end of the day, it can still reject it. Although the sheer weight, volume and sophistication of commercial propaganda may be worrying, we should be reassured by the fact that one of the first words learned by human children everywhere is 'No'.

13 | Conclusion

In a short story called *Children May be Wiser than their Elders*, Leo Tolstoy tells of two little girls, Malasha and Akulka, who have a quarrel when Malasha inadvertently stamps in a puddle and makes Akulka's best frock dirty. Malasha is seized and punished by Akulka's mother. When Malasha's mother sees her daughter being beaten, she attacks Akulka's mother and before long a full-scale row involving every peasant in the village is raging. The peace-making words of Akulka's grandmother are ignored. Meanwhile, Akulka begins to dig a channel leading from the pool of water, and Malasha, intrigued, joins her; the little stream created by the two girls runs into the middle of the warring adults, followed by the two laughing children, their quarrel forgotten. The old grandmother declares to the grown-ups:

> Here you are gathered together to fight about these same little girls, yet they themselves have long ago forgotten the whole matter, and are playing together in peace and goodwill. They are wiser than you.

I am often reminded of this story when reading the things that adults say about children and television. Since Mary Whitehouse, in 1967, expressed her horror at her pupils losing their Christian principles, there has been a steady stream of adults, many of whom do not seem to watch very much television, earnestly pontificating about the terrible damage that television can and does do to children, while children, unnoticed and unconsulted, get on with enjoying their own programmes and activities, and with growing up. The girls Mary Whitehouse wrote about are likely to be respectable wives and mothers with teenage children of their own now; if they are, I hope that their families have had as much pleasure, relaxation and information from television as ours has. Twenty-one eventful years have elapsed since 1967 and it is doubtful whether those of us who were subjected to the 'sub-Christian' horrors of the Sixties have given them a moment's thought since, unlike Mrs. Whitehouse, who is still pontificating about films and programmes she has not seen.

For those of us Christians who have grown older and, hopefully, wiser since then, there have been worse things to worry about, including the very much more sub-Christian horrors of the 1980s – the dismantling of the Welfare State and the glorification of greed. This glorification of greed, in the guise of the encouragement of enterprise, may prove far more threatening to the relationship between children and television than anything transmitted in the dear dead Sixties. When profitability becomes the only criterion for producing television programmes, children, with their not very profitable needs for specially made programmes and performers, will get short shrift. This process has already begun, with Michael Grade, Chief Executive of Channel 4, dropping regular children's programmes from the channel, and Greg Dyke of London Weekend complaining at the 1988 Edinburgh Television Festival that ITV's children's programmes were too costly and had 'very little effect' (i.e. they didn't pull in large audiences).

As I hope some of the evidence and arguments in this book have shown, the 'effects' of television are not measurable only by counting heads in the audience. What children get out of television (and what they bring to it) is often quite different from what adults assume they get out of it. Adults may wrangle away, like Tolstoy's peasants, about the damage being done to the young; Greg Dyke and his accountants may resent the lack of cost-effectiveness in entertaining and educating the small audience of *Rainbow*. Other adults may agree or disagree. Meanwhile, small children go on faithfully liking TV puppets and songs, watching people make things and sitting on older people's laps during *EastEnders* or the afternoon racing. School-age children go on being devoted to cartoons, action adventures, family dramas like soap opera, exciting stories, silly jokes, collecting stickers and playing Thundercats or Neighbours, just as their parents played Cowboys and Indians based on the Westerns we saw at the cinema.

Lord Rees-Mogg, Douglas Hurd, Richard Ingrams, those well-known experts on child-rearing, will go on using their privileged platforms in the press to declare that young people are, in Ingrams's words, 'rendered apathetic morons by gazing night after night at the telly and thereby becoming utterly indifferent to other people's needs' (*The Observer* 10 July 1988). Meanwhile children just get on with their lives, part of which is the business of watching television – developing tastes for more serious informative programmes; losing interest in *Top of the Pops* though perhaps not yet *Neighbours*. Comedy, particularly comedy with an anarchical edge such as *The Young Ones* or *Blackadder*, starts to have an irresistible attraction; individual interests like sport, or fashion, or politics, or music begin to claim different groups of young people. Children cease to be 'children' and start becoming part of different 'minority audiences'. Television is a part of growing up, probably quite an important part; often, as I have argued, a beneficial part, which we have hardly begun to take seriously, so busy are we looking for the 'bad effects' and for something other than ourselves to blame for the cruelty and selfishness in our society.

I have argued in this book that television serves many useful purposes for children. It informs them; it helps to structure their lives; it gives them common interests with their friends and with other members of the family; it provides an occasion for family togetherness, discussion and sometimes argument. It gives them ideas for play and work; it can be used and studied at school. Above all, children use television primarily as entertainment – a valuable and valued form of leisure-time activity which they can choose to do or not to do. Of course, what and how much children watch needs to be controlled to some extent by parents; but the sooner children are encouraged to make choices and discriminations for themselves, the better it will be for them in the long run, even though their choices may seem quite inexplicable to more sophisticated grown-up tastes.

Children are different from adults; their understanding and knowledge is in many ways more limited (and in some ways less so – watch any child enthusiastically tackling a computer keyboard and then watch an adult's nervous fumblings). Children's tastes are broader and, to us, cruder. But children need to be children. They need to be allowed to enjoy what to us seem garish and vulgar stories and playthings; they need Enid Blyton and Roger the Dodger, and Masters of the Universe and My Little Pony. These can be the stepping stones to the appreciation of more complex and subtle ways of telling stories and representing the world, which become appropriate as children grow more mature. At the moment television in Britain broadly provides this mix for children – a mix ranging from cartoons like *Scooby Doo* to drama serials like *Chronicles of Narnia*; from magazine programmes like *Going Live* to serious and informative documentaries such as *Newsround Extras*. There are some gaps in children's provision, for instance for children around ten to 13. Pre-school television, too, is beginning to seem threatened – and TV still has to come to terms with the fact that children of two and three years old *do* watch television and their tastes, and limitations, need to be considered too.

In arguing that 'television is good for your kids' I am emphatically not lining up with the false prophets of children's 'needs' who argue (as Michael Grade did on *Right to Reply* in April 1988) that ten-year-olds like pop music and that because *The Chart Show* is popular with this age group therefore the needs of ten-year-olds are being met. The pop music industry has a glamour and slickness that will always attract children during the pre-teen phase; but its approach is almost totally commercial. To enjoy it, children need to buy records, clothes and magazines. In our family, we know better than to knock it; it is acceptable so long as it doesn't dominate our children's lives completely, as it might do if television offered nothing else for what programme-planners like to call 'the youth audience' (or what might more appropriately be called 'the youth market'). My eight-year-old daughter has a bedroom plastered with portraits of Kylie Minogue (the pop-singing star of *Neighbours*) and she plays the tape of the Minogue album for hours at a time. We are prepared to tolerate this so long as Elinor is still happy to get covered in mud in Epping Forest, to listen to the occasional track of Mozart or Ella Fitzgerald in the car and to wear sensible shoes that fit. Pop culture is popular with children and it would be a total killjoy who tried to wrest it away from them. But it doesn't need television to promote its interests; it has vast sums at its disposal to do this job for itself.

Nor do I ally myself with the equally false prophets like Neil Postman who argue that, because ten-year-olds are being encouraged to enjoy adult popular music and fashions, ten-year-olds therefore no longer exist. Ten-year-olds do exist and they are very different from 15- or 20-year-olds. Some ten-year-old girls, for example, are just beginning their adolescent growth spurt, while some ten-year-old boys are as much as two years away from theirs. Ten-year-olds are still small and undeveloped and, as such, vulnerable and in need of adult protection. In our society, at ten, children are on the verge of one of the big social changes in their lives: the transfer to secondary school. Hence, school performance may loom large in their lives. Their peers, particularly same-sex friends, are extremely important to them, whereas the opposite sex is not. They still see their parents as powerful and, hopefully, admirable, although conflict more frequently happens. The family group is still important – older siblings may be idolised, younger ones despised, or a sibling may be the most precious confidant in their lives. I could go on listing the many ways in which ten-year-olds are, and for the foreseeable future, will continue to be, children, not adults, nor teenagers. But the point should be obvious: programmes for this age group should reflect the characteristics and interests of this age group. Pop music and pop culture do not do that – and nor do 'family shows', which in many European countries and the United States, pass for 'children's television'.

One of the most often quoted remarks of the French critic Roland Barthes is that 'a critic needs also to be a fan'. Many critics of television are obviously not fans – television clearly does not serve the useful, positive and happy purposes for them that it has served for us, and for some of the other people I have described in this book. Many critics of television and, even more, researchers into television, claim objectivity: they are seeking to establish 'effects' or 'relationships' between television and children in a completely impartial way. I do not believe it is possible for anyone to be impartial about television. When 98 per cent of households own a television set and when most people under the age of 20 have grown up with television, we all have experience of living with television; we all have a view of it, and a view on it. Feelings about television help to determine choice of research topics. Why, for instance, is there so much research on violence? Why is there a lot of research on sex role stereotyping? Why is there concern about television's effects on learning? Why is there such a mass of market research on the kinds of commercials children like?

In the case of violence and sexism, the answer has to be that these are emotive subjects about which people *feel* strongly. People who are not fans, who cannot surrender to the enjoyment of popular media, or understand how other people can enjoy things that they don't, are also much more interested in finding out the bad news about children and television than in finding the good news. People generally are often much more interested in bad news than in good news, as every tabloid newspaper knows. Thus, books and articles which point out the terrible effects of television on children, which tell us that we are corrupting, depraving, destroying and doping our children every time we leave them in front of the box, tend to appeal to the gloomy pessimist lurking in many grown-up hearts. The enormous negative bias in most of the research topics and literature about children and television cannot be accidental.

The other research areas I've mentioned above are also areas in which there are large institutions, like the education system, or the toy industry, with vested interests in finding out specific answers to specific questions about children and television. Such vested interests are sources of research funding, but the answers provided by this kind of research will not give the whole complex picture of children's relationship to television over the whole period of childhood. Thus many of the statements made about the relationship between children and television cannot strictly be called comprehensive. The evidence from correspondence to the television companies quoted in Chapter 10 further suggests that many adults seem to like being depressing – they only write to the BBC or ITV when they have something to complain about. But children don't. Children write to praise. Children like television because, in the words of the children in Patricia Palmer's Australian study, it provides 'fun' and 'excitement'. Children like to enjoy themselves. They like *Neighbours* because people are nice to each other, and they like advertisements best when they are 'funny'. Children, in other words, are fans – and have thus made the first step towards being critics too, if only we could have the sense to see it, and encourage it.

I believe that people writing about, or researching into, television, should declare their interests. If they don't watch television, or watch it and don't like it, they should say so. I am a fan, and I did research into television's effects on how people learn, partly because I was a fan – because I believed those effects were there, and were worth investigating. When I was a child, I was a fan too; in those pre-TV days, I was criticised for 'always having my nose in a book'. I loved reading, and I loved going to the pictures, and, when we got a TV set, I loved watching that. When I had children of my own, some of my happiest memories are of times when we watched television together – or when they and a crowd of their cousins and friends watched television together. From the earliest days of joining in with Brian Cant and Jonathan Cohen on *Play School*, to more recent, and more sophisticated times, when our older children and their friends repeated word for word the whole of one episode of *Blackadder*, improvising the sharing out of parts as they went along, to a group of astonished adults, television has been a constant stimulus and delight to my children. It certainly hasn't held them back in their studies, nor in their appreciation of other cultural forms. Both the older children took exams at their comprehensive school in the summer of 1988 – one took A level, the other GCSE. Along with other excellent grades, both got an A for English. I am sure that their lifelong experience as fans contributed to the critical abilities reflected in these exam marks.

Television isn't an unmixed blessing and every family has to find ways of living with it that meet the many disparate requirements of family life. As I was writing this book, I became over-sensitive to my children's televiewing habits; far more likely to rush into the sitting room on a fine afternoon and upbraid the children for sitting gormlessly in front of *Coppers and Co*, just in case Marie Winn, or one of her devotees, should turn up and find us all plugged in. They found this amusing – and went along with it. There are certainly scenes and films that I would not be happy for my children to see and I was indignant when Kathy, a character in *EastEnders*, was allowed to describe graphically her experience of being raped at 7.30 in the evening when my younger children were watching. Nevertheless, these problems are not insuperable. As parents, we have always remained in ultimate control of what is seen on television by our children and, so far, have been able to deal with any distress caused by programmes – distress which it is not always possible to anticipate, because children vary in what they find upsetting. The good we have received from television far outweighs the bad; it even includes some of these experiences of distress.

I hope that British television companies will be allowed to go on providing programmes that do not just pull in the largest audiences for the richest advertisers, but which recognise their responsibilities as a public service. I hope that when deregulation comes, and we are given a 'choice' of a dozen or more channels beamed in from Europe and America, via space, that this 'choice' will continue to include a range of different programme types, for children (and adults) of all ages. I hope that people will be found who want to work for children in television, who can accept and enjoy the responsibility of turning young fans into critics. I hope that my grandchildren will have as many positive experiences of growing up with television as my children have had. I hope that they won't find this book among the family heirlooms and wonder what on earth poor old Gran was on about when she wrote about drama and documentary and news and film and political debate and schools programmes. I hope they won't be startled that she seemed to believe that a medium they only know as 18 channels of commercially sponsored pap was once considered 'good for your kids'.

References, bibliography and addresses

References are listed by chapter and preceded by the number of the page on which they occur.

Chapter 2: The first side of the partnership: children

13. Vurpillot, E. and Zoberman, N. (1956), 'Rôle des indices communs et des indices distincts dans la differentiation perceptive', Acta psychologica, 24, 49, quoted in Jorg, S., (1978), 'Characteristic features of visual perception development up to the beginning of school', *Perception, Development, Communication*, Fernsehen und Bildung, K.G. Saur, New York.

14. Smith, R., Anderson, D.R. and Fisher, C. (1985), 'Young children's comprehension of montage', *Child Development*, 56, 962-971.

14. Kodaira, S.I. (1987), *Children and Television: A study of new TV programmes for children, based on the pilot of an animated production*, NHK Broadcasting Culture Research Institute Report.

15. Ball, J. (1983), *Plays for Laughs*, Penguin, London.

16. Egly, M. (1973), 'Téléniger', *Dossiers Pedagogiques*, 1, 2-5, quoted in P.M. Greenfield, (1984) *Mind and Media*, Fontana, London.

17. Messenger Davies, M., Lloyd A. and Scheffler E. (1987) *Baby Language*, Unwin Hyman, London.

18. Newport, E.L., Gleitman, H. and Gleitman, L.R. (1977), 'Mother I'd rather do it myself: some effects and non-

effects of maternal speech style', in Snow, C. and Ferguson, C. (Eds), *Talking to Children*, Cambridge University Press.

18. Rydin, I. (1976), *Children's Understanding of Television: Pre-school children's perception of an informative programme*, Swedish Broadcasting Corporation, Audience and Programme Research Department.

18. Alwitt, L.F., Anderson, D.R., Lorch, E.P. and Levin, S.R. (1980), 'Pre-school children's visual attention to attributes of television', *Human Communication Research*, 7, 52-67, quoted in Bryant, J. and Anderson, D.R. (Eds) (1983), *Children's Understanding of Television*, Academic Press, London.

19. Gerhartz-Franck, I. (1955), 'Neber Geschenogestaltungen in der Auffassung von Filmen durch Kinder', (Leipzig, Barth), quoted in Noble, G. (1975), *Children in Front of the Small Screen*, Sage/Constable, London.

19. Acker, S.R. and Tiemans, R.K. (1981), 'Children's perceptions of changes in size of televised images', *Human Communication Research*, Summer 1981, 7, 4, 340-346.

19. *The IBA Code of Advertising Standards and Practice*, (1987), Independent Broadcasting Authority, London.

20. Messenger Davies, M. (1987), *An Investigation into Certain Effects of Television Camera Technique on Cognitive Processing*, unpublished PhD thesis, North East London Polytechnic.

21. Frith, U. and Robson, J.E. (1975), 'Perceiving the language of films', *Perception*, 4, 97-103.

24. Noble, G. (1975), *Children in Front of the Small Screen*, Sage/Constable, London.

25. Salomon, G. (1977), 'Effects of encouraging Israeli mothers to co-observe *Sesame Street* with their five-year-olds', *Child Development*, 48, 1146-1151.

26. Jaglom, L.M. and Gardner, H. (Eds) (1981) 'The pre-school television viewer as anthropologist', in Kelly, H. and Gardner, H. (Eds) (1981), *Viewing Children through Television*, Jossey Bass, San Francisco.

29. Wober, J.M. (1986), *Patterns of Viewing Perceptions*

and Personality amongst Children: some preliminary findings, IBA Research Department Working Paper, quoted in Woolfson, R. 'I want to be like Mr T.', *Nursery World* 5 November 1987.

Chapter 3: The other side of the partnership: television

31. Dunn, G. (1977), *The Box in the Corner*, Macmillan, London.
41. BBC Broadcasting Department (1984), *Daily Life in the 1980s*.
42. Root, J. (1986), *Open the Box*, Comedia, London.
42. Wober, J.M. (1986), *Children and How Much They View*, Discussion Paper, IBA, London.

Chapter 4: Television – corrupter of the young?

53. de Villiers, P. and de Villiers, J. (1979), *Early Language*, Fontana/Open Books, London.
53. Messenger Davies, M., Lloyd, E. and Scheffler, A. (1987) op cit.
54. Murphy, C. (1983), *Talking about Television: Opportunities for language development in young children*, IBA, London.
54. Gunter, B. and Wober, M. (1988), *Violence on Television: What the Viewers Think*, John Libbey, London.
55. Anderson, D.R. and Lorch, E.P. (1983), 'Looking at television: action or reaction?', in Bryant, J. and Anderson, D.R. (Eds), *Children's Understanding of Television*, Academic Press, London.
56. Dorr, A. (1986), *Television and Children: A Special Medium for a Special Audience*, Sage, London.
56. Noble, G. (1975) op cit.
62. Salomon, G. (1981), *Interaction of Media, Cognition and Learning*, Jossey Bass, London.

62. Pezdek, K. (1977), 'Cross modality integration of sentence and picture memory', *Journal of Experimental Psychology*, 3, 515-524.

62. Smith, R., Anderson, D.R. and Fisher, C. (1985), 'Young children's comprehension of montage', *Child Development*, 56, 962-971.

62. Messenger Davies, M. (1987) op cit.

62. Richards, M. (1980), *Infancy*, Harper and Row, London.

Chapter 5: Television and the mind

65. Halloran, J.D. (1974), in Homberg, E. (Ed), *Pre-school Children and Television*, K.G. Saur, New York.

65. Murphy, C. (1983), op cit

66. Noble, G. (1975), op cit.

67. Hodge, R. and Tripp, D. (1986), *Children and Tele-vision*, Polity Press, Oxford.

69. Richman, N., Stevenson, J. and Graham, P.J. (1982), *Pre-school to School: A Behavioural Study*, Academic Press, London.

69. Huston, A.C. and Wright, J.C. (1983), 'Children's processing of television: the informative functions of formal features', in Bryant, J. and Anderson, D.R. (Eds), *Children's Understanding of Television*, Academic Press, London.

70. Calvert, S.L., Huston, A.C., Watkins, B.A. and Wright, J.C. (1982), 'The effects of selective attention to television forms on children's comprehension of content', *Child Development*, 53, 601-610.

71. Kodaira, S.I. (1987), op cit.

71. Wright, J.C. et al, (1980), 'Children's selective attention to television forms: effects of salient and informative production features as functions of age and viewing experience'. Paper presented at the Meeting of the International Communication Association, Mexico.

72. Brown, L.K. (1986), *Taking Advantage of Media*, Routledge and Kegan Paul, London.

73. Messenger Davies, M. (1987) op cit.

75. Chandler, M.J., Greenspan, S. and Barenboim, C. (1973), 'Judgements of intentionality in response to video-taped and verbally presented moral dilemmas: the medium is the message', *Child Development*, 44, 315-320.

78. Murphy, C. and Wood, D.J. (1982), 'Learning through media: a comparison of four- to eight-year-old children's responses to filmed and pictorial instruction', *International Journal of Behavioural Development*, 5, 195-216.

80. Pinder, R. (1987), *Why Don't Teachers Teach Like They Used To?*, Hilary Shipman, London.

80. Berry, C. and Clifford, B.R. (1987), *Learning from Television News* IBA/North East London Polytechnic.

81. Messenger Davies, M. (1989), 'Why can people jump higher on the moon? A study of what children learned from a children's TV programme', *Journal of Educational Television* 15, 1.

83. Cook, T.D. et al (1975), *Sesame Street Revisited*, Russell Sage Foundation, New York.

83. Salomon, G. (1981) op cit.

84. Messenger Davies, M., Berry, C. and Clifford, B.R. (1985), 'Unkindest cuts? Some effects of picture editing on recall of television news information', *Journal of Educational Television*, 11, 2, 85-98.

Chapter 6: Television and violence

85. Curteis, I. (1988), 'Let's knock some sense into the programme makers', *Evening Standard*, 3 February 1988.

85. Messenger Davies, M. (1985), 'Who says TV is bad for you?', *The Listener*, 21 November 1985.

86. Gunter, B. and Wober, M. (1988) op cit.

86. Bandura, A. (1969), 'Social learning theory of identifi-

catory processes', in Goslin (Ed), *Handbook of Socialization Theory and Research*, Rand McNally, Chicago.

86. Durkin, K. (1985), *Television, Sex Roles and Children*, Open University Press, Milton Keynes.

87. Wober, J.M., Reardon, G. and Fazal, S. (1987), *Personality, Character Aspirations and Patterns of Viewing among Children*, IBA Research Paper, London.

87. Lefkowitz, M.M., Eron, L.D., Walder, L.O. and Huesmann, L.R., (1977), *Growing up to be Violent*, Pergamon, New York.

87. Singer, J. and Singer, D. (1979), 'Television-viewing, family style and aggressive behavior in pre-school children', American Association for the Advancement of Science Symposium, quoted in Green, M. (ed), *Violence and the American Family*.

89. Charren, P., Paper about American Action for Children's Television (ACT), given to BFI Television and the Family Conference, London, 1987.

89. Wober, J.M. (1986) op cit (*Nursery World*).

91. Hodge, R. and Tripp D. (1986) op cit.

92. Gerbner, G., Gross, L. , Morgan, M. and Signiorelli, N. (1982), 'Charting the mainstream; television's contribution to political orientations', *Journal of Communication*, 30, 37-47.

92. Gunter, B. and Wakshlag, J. (1986), 'Television viewing and perceptions of crime among London residents', Paper given to International Television Studies Conference, London, 1986.

92. Wober, J.M. (1987), *British Children, Their Television Viewing and Confidence in the Face of Crime*, IBA Research Paper, London.

92. Noble, G. (1983), 'Social Learning from Everyday Television', in Howe, M.J.A. (Ed), *Learning from Television: Psychological and Educational Research*, Academic Press, London.

95. Barlow, G. and Hill, A. (1985), *Video Violence and Children*, Hodder and Stoughton, London.

Chapter 7: Television and social attitudes

101. Whitehouse, M. (1967), *Cleaning Up TV*, Blandford, London.

101. Ferguson, R. (1984), 'Black Blue Peter',in Masterman, L. (Ed), *Television Mythologies*, Comedia, London.

105. Buckingham, D. (1984), 'The whites of their eyes: a case study in responses to educational television', in Straker-Welds, M. (Ed), *Education for a Multicultural Society*, Bell and Hyman, London

108. Newell, D. (1988), 'Television viewing among Afro-Caribbeans living in the United Kingdom', Paper given to the International Television Studies Conference, London, 1988.

112. Knill, B.J., Peach, M., Pursey G., Gilpin, P. and Perloff, R.M. (1981), 'Still typecast after all these years: sex role portrayals in television advertising', *International Journal of Women's Studies*, 4, 497-506.

112. Manstead, A.R.S. and McCulloch, C. (1981), 'Sex role stereotyping in British television advertisements', *British Journal of Social Psychology*,, 20, 171-180.

112. Winick, C., Williamson, L.G., Chuzmir, S.F. and Winick, M.P. (1973), *Children's Television Commercials: A Content Analysis*, Praeger, New York.

113. BBC Broadcasting Research Department Report on Children's Television Presenters, (1986).

113. Gunter, B. (1986), *Television and Sex Role Stereotyping*, John Libbey, London.

115. Durkin, K. (1983), *Sex Roles and Children's Television*, Report to the IBA.

116. Durkin, K. (1985) *Television, Sex Roles and Children*, Open University Press, Milton Keynes.

Chapter 8: Television in the classroom

118. Murdock, G. and Phelps, G. (1973), *Mass Media and the Secondary School*, Schools Council, Macmillan.

119. BBC Broadcasting Research Department Survey on Listening and Viewing in UK Schools, (1987).

127. Lusted, D. (1985), 'A history of suspicion: educational attitudes to television', in Lusted, D. and Drummond, P. (Eds), *TV and Schooling*, BFI/University of London Institute of Education.

127. BFI/DES National Working Party on Primary Media Education, Working Papers 1,2,3,4 (1986-8); Star Biscuits project from Working Papers Three, June 1987.

130. Greenfield, P.M. (1984), *Mind and Media*, Fontana, London.

127. Messenger Davies, M. (1987) Phd thesis, op cit.

132. Clifford, B., Messenger Davies, M., Phillips, K., Pitts, M. and White, D. (1988), 'Learning Aids: how teenagers responded to a video', *Times Educational Supplement*, 29 April 1988.

132. Neuwirth, S. (1982), 'Using television to teach story comprehension: one teacher's experience', *Television and Children*, 5, 36-38.

134. Singer, D. (1982) Paper given at conference on Children and Television, Boystown, Nebraska, 1982 quoted in P.M. Greenfield (1984), op cit.

Chapter 9: Television as entertainment

135. Melody, W.H. (1987), 'Children's television: frontier for the electronic billboard', Paper given at BFI Summer School, In Front of the Children, University of Stirling, July 1987.

136. Lusted, D. (1984), op cit.

137. Nelson, J. (1988), 'Tuned in and switched off', *New Internationalist*, February 1988.

140. Morley, D. (1986), *Family Television: Cultural Power and Domestic Leisure*, Comedia, London.

141. Dorr, A. (1986), op cit.

141. Himmelweit, H. (1958), *Television and the Child*, Oxford University Press.

142. Greenberg, S., Gunter, B. Wober, M. and Fazal, S. (1986), *Children and their Media*, IBA Research Report.

143. Pylyshyn, Z. (1973), 'What the mind's eye tells the mind's brain: a critique of mental imagery', *Psychological Bulletin*, 80, 1, 1-23.

147. Palmer, P. (1986), 'The social nature of children's television viewing', Paper presented at the International Television Studies Conference, London, 1986.

Chapter 10: Children's responses to television

160. See e.g. Shaffer, D., Meyer-Bahlburg, H.F.L. and Stockman, C.L.J. (1980) in Rutter, M. (Ed), *Scientific Foundations of Developmental Psychiatry*, Heinemann, London.

161. Buckingham, D. (1987), *Public Secrets: EastEnders and its Audience*, BFI, London.

162. Noble, G. (1983) 'Social learning from everyday television', op cit.

162. Hodge, R. and Tripp, D. (1986,) op cit.

163. Bettelheim, B. (1976) *The Uses of Enchantment*, Thames and Hudson, London.

163. Chandler, M.J. et al (1973) op cit.

Chapter 11: Television spin-offs

167. Neuman, S.B. (1986), 'Television and reading : a research synthesis', Paper given to International Television Studies Conference, London, 1986.

167. Hincks, T. and Balding, J.W. (1988), 'On the relationship between television viewing time and book reading for pleasure: the self-reported behaviour of 11- to 16-year-olds', *Reading*, 22, 1, 40-50.

172. Rotman, B. (1986), 'Toying with the audience', *The Listener*, 9 October 1986.

175. Sweeney, E. (1988), 'The child audience', Paper given at Advertising and Children seminar, held by British Toy and Hobby Manufacturers' Association at IBA, April 1988.

179. Home, A. (1987) quoted in 'Concern over screen series and toy links', *Ariel*, 2 September 1987.

Chapter 12: Children and television advertising

183. Young, B. (1984), 'New approaches to old problems: the growth of advertising literacy', Paper presented to conference on International Perspectives on Television Advertising and Children, Provence, 1984.

186. Children's Monitor, Report from The Research Business, London, January 1988.

187. Sweeney, E. (1988) op cit.

189. Martin, J. and Monk, J. (1980) *Infant Feeding*, OPCS, London.

189. Duffy, J. and Rossiter, J.R. (1975), 'The Hartford experiment: children's reactions to TV commercials in blocks at the beginning and the end of the program', Paper presented to conference on Culture and Communications, Philadelphia, 1975.

190. Rubin, R. S. (1972), 'An exploratory investigation of children's responses to commercial content of television advertising in relation to their stages of cognitive development', unpublished Phd dissertation, University of Massachusetts.

190. Messenger Davies, M. et al (1985) 'Unkindest cuts?'. op cit.

191. Atkin, C. (1975), 'Effects of television advertising on children – first year experimental evidence', Michigan State University.

191. Adler, R.P., Lesser, G.S., Meringoff, L.K., Robertson, T.S. Rossiter, J.R. and Ward, S. (1980), *The Effects of Television Advertising on Children*, Lexington, Massachusetts.

198. Wober, J.M. (1986), *Advertisements, Children and Christmas Time: Some Patterns of Attitudes*, IBA Research Report.
199. Millwood, Y. (1988), 'Why a code?' Paper given at Advertising and Children, seminar held by British Toy and Hobby Manufacturers' Association at IBA, London.

Bibliography

Adler, R.P., Lesser, G.S., Meringoff, L.K., Robertson, T.S., Rossiter, J.R. and Ward, S. (1980), *The Effects of Television Advertising on Children*, Lexington, Massachusetts.

Bettelheim, B. (1976), *The Uses of Enchantment*, Thames and Hudson, London.

Brown, L.K. (1986), *Taking Advantage of Media*, Routledge and Kegan Paul, London.

Brown, R.(Ed) (1974), *Children and Television*, Collier Macmillan, London.

Bryant, J. and Anderson, J.R. *Children's Understanding of Television: Research on Attention and Comprehension*, Academic Press, London.

Buckingham, D. (1987), *Public Secrets: EastEnders and its Audience*, BFI, London.

Burnett, Frances Hodgson, (1911), *The Secret Garden*, Puffin, London.

Cohen, P. and Gardner, C. (1982), *It Ain't Half Racist, Mum*, Comedia, London.

Dorr, A. (1986), *Children and Television: A Special Medium for a Special Audience*, Sage, London.

Dunn, G. (1977), *The Box in the Corner*, Macmillan, London.

Durkin, K. (1985), *Television, Sex Roles and Children*, Open University Press, London.

Greenfield, P.M. (1984), *Mind and Media*, Fontana, London.

Gunter, B. (1986), *Television and Sex Role Stereotyping*, John Libbey, London.

Hardyment, C. (1983), *Dream Babies*, Jonathan Cape, London.

Hodge, R. and Tripp, D. (1986), *Children and Television*, Polity Press, Oxford.

Howe, M.J.A. (Ed) (1983), *Learning from Television: Psychological and Educational Research*, Academic Press, London.

Laski, M. (Ed) (1947), *Victorian Tales for Girls*, Pilot Press, London.

Lusted, D. (Ed) (1985), *TV and Schooling*, BFI/London University Institute of Education, London.

Masterman, L. (Ed), (1984), *Television Mythologies*, Comedia, London.

Masterman, L. (1980), *Teaching Television*, Macmillan, London.

Messenger Davies, M., Lloyd, E. and Scheffler, A. (1987), *Baby Language*, Unwin Hyman, London.

Morley, D. (1986), *Family Television: Cultural Power and Domestic Leisure*, Comedia, London.

Noble, G. (1975), *Children in Front of the Small Screen*, Sage/Constable, London.

Postman, N. (1985), *The Disappearance of Childhood*, W.H. Allen, London.

Root, J. (1986), *Open the Box*, Comedia, London.

Salomon, G., (1981), *Interaction of Media, Cognition and Learning*, Jossey Bass, London.

Simpson, P. (Ed) (1987), *Parents Talking Television*, Comedia/Methuen, London.

Straker-Welds, M.(Ed) (1984), *Education for a Multicultural Society*, Bell and Hyman, London.

Wober, M. and Gunter, B. (1988), *Television and Social Control*, Gower, Aldershot.

Useful addresses

BBC Children's Department, BBC Television Centre, Wood Lane, London W12 8QT.

BBC TV Schools Broadcasting, Villiers House, The Broadway, London W5 2PA.

BFI Education Dept, 21 Stephen St., London W1P 1PL, for booklists on film and television, and regional addresses for media education contacts.

BFI Film and Video Library, address as above (for hire of *Open the Box* video and other media education video material).

British Action for Children's Television, c/o Philip Simpson, Head of Education, British Film Institute, 21 Stephen St., London W1P 1PL.

Broadcasting Standards Council, 5-8 The Sanctuary, London SW1P 3JS.

Independent Broadcasting Authority, 70 Brompton Rd, London SW3 1EY (for all inquiries concerning ITV and Channel 4 programmes, and IBA research, plus regional addresses for the ITV companies).

Index

Index

Index